MW01169460

DESIGN

A Woman's Ultimate Guide to
Getting It Right
Keeping It Tight
-and-
Claiming Your Queendom

Lisa King

"If faith, the size of a
mustard seed is all that is
needed to believe that all
your dreams are possible-
then a little audacity is
energy needed to
transform those dreams
into reality." -Lisa K.

www.ALittleAudacity.com

BY DESIGN

A Woman's Ultimate Guide to:
Getting it Right, Keeping it Tight
and Claiming Your Queendom

Lisa King

Printed in the United States of America

A Little Audacity, Inc.

New York, NY

www.ALittleAudacity.com

Graphics by Kendall Word

For:

June, Mother Extraordinaire and #1 Supporter

My Best Friend Tashica, for never doubting me- ever

and the Lovely Ladies of the Sassy Sistahs Book Club

Thank you to my team of powerful women:

Chanel, Tuso and Nanette

Dedicated to:

Isaiah, mommy loves you so much and Rick, thank you for being a mark in time.

Table of Contents:

CLAIM YOUR QUEENDOM

La Femme Devine, Poetry by Lisa K.

Confidence is like hair. It grows stronger with proper conditioning." Marshawn Evans

PREFACE

What if I told that I have information that could make you more confident, bolder, healthier, happier and even more attractive than you are, right here and right now?

Would you want me to share?
Would you really want to know?
Of course you would!

If the idea of being a self-assured, self-reliant, and stylish woman to boot is peaking your curiosity, then this book was written just for you.

By Design is a guide for the modern woman who has gone through some heartache, some hardship or gotten a little carried away with life and needs to be reminded of her crown. In this book, you'll discover ways to invoke your royal presence and stake your claim in the world.

You may have read the title and thought: *By Design*? Oh great, another self-help book… just what I need! But *By Design* is much more than just a self-help book. When the principles shared in this book are applied to your life, it will completely change your outlook on who are and the way you show up in the world.

Confused? Ok, well let me explain.

You're probably thinking, *By Design*? *Design* what? And for who? The answer is simple -- YOU.

My question to you is... Are you a Designed Woman?

If you're thinking about it.... clearly you're not - at least not yet.
But who is this Designed Woman, I speak of? What does she do?

Well, we all know her. She's that woman that other women want to be. As young girls, we dream about becoming her one day. She is confident, bold, beautiful and goal-oriented. She's a businesswoman calling the shots. She's a mom holding down the family. She may be going to school, working a 9-5 job or launching her new business. What ever she's doing - she's making it happen on *her* terms and loving every minute of her journey.

You can catch her singing *Chaka Khan's " I'm every woman. Its all in meeeeeee. Everything you need done baby, I do it naturally, ooh ohh ohhhhh"*

She is the Ultimate Woman. Let's dive into that a bit.

This Ultimate Woman has one thing that the average woman doesn't have -- a "presence of mind". This is a woman who chooses to live life on her terms. She *creates* her reality because she isn't *waiting* for a new job, a new partner, a better situation or a big break to give her what she needs. She uses what she has - to get what she needs and she isn't afraid to demand what she wants. She acknowledges her reality and chooses to expand her playing fields, always and in all ways. Self-motivated and determined, she lives out her dreams each and every day of her life. Her motivation and internal focus guarantees her a life that is to be envied by those who don't claim their Queendoms.

Still with me? Good. Keep going and by the end of this book, you will have all the information you need to become the woman that other women look at and say:

"That's the Woman to be."
"That Woman is so damned lucky."
"How does she find the time to do it all?"
"She's superwoman, for sure."

Some will ask you how you do it. Some will hate from the sidelines. Whichever way it goes, by the end of this book you'll know that you are *exactly* who you are to be. Why? Because you'll have the knowledge, tools and that extra oomph you'll need to design it that way.

You deserve every blessing that's coming your way and I am so excited to get you started on your journey! So get ready for a fun, sassy and informative read geared to transform your self-perception and rekindle the passion and excitement of living your life the way you choose to. Your life is yours to design! Are you ready? Lets go!

BEFORE WE BEGIN

Lets make a pact to each other that ego as well as self-doubt will be put away. In order to get the most from this guide, you must

- Be unapologetically honest with yourself and
- Be completely open to change.

Some of what you're are about to learn, you'll think you know already, and that is probably true. But… to know something is one thing - to actually live it out is an entirely different ball game. With an open mind and the willingness to live an absolutely amazing life, by any means necessary, you are about enter a world of transformation. May your journey to absolute fabulousness be enlightening and humbling.

THE READING PROCESS

This book aims to bring forth your ultimate woman. At the end of each chapter, I've included thought-provoking questions and/or action-exercises to get the transformation process started and to keep it going. However, bear in mind that this advice is about changing the way you *think* and encourages *changing* your lifestyle - so please TAKE YOUR TIME. Do not speed through this experience because "You can't rush fabulous honey!"

Should you like more guidance or one-on-one coaching, please visit: www.alitlleaudacity.com for a free online guide which incorporates all the exercises in this book as well as bi-weekly blogs to keep you motivated and on track with your goals.

Have additional questions or comments? Send them to info@alittleaudacity.com.

THE HISTORY- how and why did this book happen?

On reflection, I've unknowingly been writing this book over the course of a few years. I was in my late 20's, pregnant and holding on to a relationship that had put life into me (literally) but had managed to suck the live energy from me in the process.

Let's take a moment to get my sad story out of the way so we can get back to the FAB.

So there I was on the bathroom floor, crying uncontrollably and 8 months pregnant with his child. It was over and I knew it. I cried because I didn't see it coming. I didn't know where I went wrong because I loved him with all my heart. I fought my friends. I went against my family. I defended him and tried to convince them of what we had in each other. Yet still, after all that I had put on the line for our 'love 'here I was, broken and still wanting him to save me. So I cried and waited and waited... He didn't come. I cried louder, harder- ripping the hurt from my body, hoping that he would somehow be moved by my pain and come in to pick me up from the floor. He didn't. With the sound of the front door shutting, and the lock clicking, I was hit with the truth. I was officially alone.

Rick was my other half on so many levels. It was like we were the same person at times. I met him when I was 14 years old at our neighborhood YMCA. His big brother owned a clothing store, which doubled up as a hip-hop gathering spot next door to the YMCA, called Hard Core. It was where all the aspiring rappers in the city would meet up and have MC battles. There was always a crowd outside the shop, sometimes even video crews ready to capture New York's next big rapper before stardom hit.

Rick was there with his brother Barry. Everyone knew Barry. He had created a name for himself in the neighborhood by constantly flashing money around and driving around in the kinds of exotic cars that my young, impressionable 14-year old eyes had only seen on television. Lord only knows what he had done to gain so much respect or rather, fear, in the neighborhood but no one dared to rob him.

As I passed by the shop one day, heading to cheerleading practice, Barry called out to me. Rick was with him and he was a cutie. He was a tall, light-skinned, brown-eyed brother with a slim build and a handsome face. On top of that, he had the thickest hair I had ever seen on a boy. *Definitely* something to look at…

"Hey Big Booty Lisa, I want to introduce you to my brother, Rick" said Barry, teasingly.

Rolling my eyes and waving him off, I said "Whatever Barry, anyways" and extended my hand to Rick with a sweet "hello".

To my surprise, Rick looked at my hand with slight disgust and barely at me as he shook my hand. He then mumbled something incoherent before turning away and shouting "peace out" over his shoulder.

I stood there shocked for a moment but I quickly recovered because clearly something was wrong with him. I was Lisa, one of the prettiest girls in the neighborhood with a body that already at 14 years old, looked as if it would have my dad reaching for his shotgun in no time. The truth was that I had no real interest in having a boyfriend at that time. But it seemed like my nonchalant attitude made the boys (and unfortunately some grown men), even more interested in me. I was a prize and I knew it.

"What was up with that?" I asked Barry, not really caring about the answer.

"Oh, my bro is just a bit shy around beautiful women. Trust me, he likes you -- he told me so right before I called you over," he said laughing.

"Okaaay, whatever", I said, bid him farewell and continued on my merry way to cheerleading practice.

Over the years, I routinely saw Rick every summer, mainly because we went to different high schools -- and the summertime was the only time where you could catch everybody and their mamas out and about enjoying the weather. We gradually warmed up to each other with head nods and forced Hellos at first. Until one evening, I was at the YMCA hosting their Friday Night Teen Center. This is where all the teens from the neighborhood and neighboring hoods came out to have dance contest, listen to music and hang out with each other. It was a safe haven for the most part so that kids had somewhere to go instead of hanging out in the street.

You were everything if you were one of the elite kids who got to host the Friday Night Jams. I was at the front door with the security guard giving him the go-ahead on who could come in first and who had to wait because they looked "suspicious". To my surprise, Rick walked in the doors and our eyes met briefly. He was standing in line and I silently chuckled to myself because my, my, my, how the tables had turned.

As he approached the front of the line, I couldn't help the sly smile on my face.

He walked directly up to Bobby, our security guard, to be searched. During the search, Bobby looked at me enquiringly, "is he good?". I shook my head, No. Bobby, being the friendly type, didn't ever refuse anyone access -- he simply asked them to step aside and wait. Usually, kids would be either get a stern warning from the Programs Director about keeping the peace or they would get tired of waiting and leave.

Aware of what was going on, and instead of waiting like a gentleman, Rick walked right up to me and demanded to speak to me. I pretended not to hear him because clearly this boy who barely acknowledged me earlier, couldn't be talking to me today.

"Lisa. I said let me talk to you for a second." The words sounded friendly enough but coming through his clenched teeth - I knew he was pissed.
"Oh, now you can speak to me?" I said.

"Yo ma, stop with the games, and lets go for a walk and talk like grown folks."

I simply replied "I'm busy" and continued checking kids into Teen Center.

Rick smiled, stepped in closer and whispered to me "I'll be nice, I just wanna tell you something."

I looked up at him knowing he was up to something but his softened tone sparked my curiosity.

I walked into Teen Center and we headed up to the second floor where it was quieter. I turned to him with fluttering eyes and sass and said, "Ok, you got in and I have work to do, so what is it?"

He began. "I've been watching you for a minute and I think you're cute."
I knew it. He likes me. Why wouldn't he just say so? I mean, really.

"You're fly and I heard you're a smart girl."
Uh, huh - Exactly. Continue.

"But I'm not trying to get with you, Lisa."
Wait. What?

"Yeah, that '*high and mighty*' attitude you walk around the neighborhood with doesn't do it for me. So, I brought you up here to tell you if I offended you in the way a shook your hand the other day -- my apologies. Let's squash the beef and be friends."

I couldn't believe him. Really Rick? No guy had ever said that to me. I caught myself and picked my jaw up off the floor. Quickly recovering after seeing the look of satisfaction on his face, I shook off my surprise and labeled this as the beginning of a cat and mouse game. If this is the game he wanted to play - then so be it. No one played it better than your girl.

"That's cool Rick. No beef. Here, take my number. We can be friends."
Got em'

Rick said he wasn't interested in me but that boy sure did call me every day. We spent hours on the phone at night and spoke about almost everything. We began to learn about each other but for the most part, we kept our distance in person. It was a secret friendship that grew into an unspoken bond and the more we shared, the stronger our bond became. Though, in our early years of friendship, we never crossed the line to engage in sexual activity, Rick quickly became my "go to" guy source for all my relationship issues and boy did I have drama! He was my shoulder to cry on at the end of my first serious relationship, a failed engagement and a marriage that lasted a whopping eight months. I was a busy girl, always in love back then, but Rick never judged. His friendship was the constant in my life during those years.

After graduating from college and splitting from a husband (who had the nerve to ask me to be a stay-at-home mom while he pursued a Masters degree), I needed a change of scenery. Being the free spirit I was, I decided to claim the life I wanted to live by moving to Florida! Why Florida, you ask... Well, I visited the state on vacation with my best friend and fell in love with the gorgeous weather and palm trees. And it didn't hurt that you could rent a two-bedroomed, two bathroom apartment with a washer and dryer for a little more than half of what it cost me to live in Brooklyn, New York.

I was a free spirit and made life decisions on a whim. I had never been the type to question the *how's* in the life - I just went for it. I was extremely secure in my ability to make it happen for myself. So from the moment I decided that Florida was where I wanted to be- it was a done deal. I quit my job, packed my bags and within three months, I was officially a Florida resident. Within two weeks, I got the first job I applied for... The transition was an easy one especially with Rick talking me through my emotional episodes. The hustle and bustle of moving out of state was exciting. I was making moves but soon after settling in to my new apartment, I realized that I was lonely. I talked to Rick all through the day but inside I knew I wanted him close to me. Our feelings for each other had grown into something more than friendship and we knew it. He was my best friend and now I wanted him to experience this new life with me. So I asked him to move to Florida and without a question, he relocated. We both knew that we were meant to be with one another and now, in our mid 20's, we made that decision -- together.

At first we were a team, living together and exploring what the state of Florida had to offer. I was 24 years old with an Engineering Degree, a gift of the gab and that "New York City" attitude, confident and bold. I was already working for a title insurance company when Rick arrived. I quickly learned the ropes and networked like a boss (although at that age I thought I was just making friends). I met a woman named Diana Albeski who owned her own real estate company and we clicked. I was intrigued by the fact she was a woman who actually owned and ran a successful businesses. Coming from Flatbush, Brooklyn, I knew women who held high positions in business, working for major corporations but I never had a met a woman who was an actual boss- signing checks and managing everything else it entailed to run a business. We socialized a few times, and I often used her husband as a notary public, passing work his way by getting him to go out to mortgage clients to witness and notarize their signatures on loan documents. It was fast and easy money for them and they appreciated the business I sent their way. Diana, being the go-getter she was,saw how successful the title insurance business was and, within a year, she opened her own title insurance agency. I was offered a position as a controller with her start-up company. I was young, eager and ready to learn it all, so I accepted the position. My self-confidence was at an all-time high. Even in my early 20's, I understood that everything was learnable. I was smart. I was a fast learner and whatever I didn't know, I found answers to with a click of the mouse and a mind that absorbed information like a sponge. I watched the flow of things and easily adapted to the cultures of organizations. I did this naturally. With my new position as Controller, I worked my behind off and with Rick as my personal coach and number 1 supporter and fan, business for the start-up was booming and I was winning.

I was well on my way to becoming a partner and I knew it. I managed the accounting books. I handled the payroll. I went out to real estate agencies and mortgage companies and solicited business from the companies. I was a social butterfly and sharp as a tack. That combination brought the clients (aka the money) in with ease. I was Diana's right hand and the complete trust she had in my judgment and abilities was apparent and she often proved it with chunky monthly bonuses. This was a wonderful time for Rick and I. He was so proud of me. Whenever we went out, he would boast about how his fiancé (yes ladies, he put a ring on it) was handling her business and showing the south what New York was about. His words gave me even more confidence and strength which deepened my love for him. With the extra income, we instantly became, for lack of a better term "hood rich". After all, we were in our mid 20's and quite frankly, we had no interest in saving money for a rainy day. So what did we do? We rented 5-bedroomed houses in Fort Lauderdale to have parties in. We drove out to Miami to party at the LIV – a high-end nightclub. Drinking and partying become a daily activity for us, for no other reason than – we could. I flew family members in for weekend and shopped for no reason. He became a sneaker head and bought old cars to repair as projects. We were the true definition of Brooklyn Heads living it up in the south. We were doing our thing and more importantly, we were happy.

Around the same time, Rick made a few new friends. During one of our club nights, Rick met some Jamaicans doing their city thing and they clicked right away. You see, Rick had a way of polarizing people. Upon meeting him, you either loved him or hated him- there was no in between. No matter what side of the fence you were on, when he spoke, he had your full attention. He was entertaining, to say the least. Well, the Jamaicans, who I'll call the J-Squad were clearly making money. I mean, their fashion wasn't loud at all but if you were familiar with high-end fashion, you definitely noticed their Louis Vuitton and Gucci belts, Louboutin red bottomed sneakers, bling watches and designer frames. Clearly, they were making money and once Rick started rolling with them, so was he.

As Rick started to bring more money into the household, things started to shift.

Slowly (exactly when I can't pinpoint) it became apparent that the more money he made and the more women paid him attention, the more he started to nibble at my self-confidence. It started with little comments pointing out some of my imperfections. He would say things like "You've got a big nose." and "You should stop perming your hair- I like natural girls." My food didn't taste as good. My skin didn't look as bright and apparently, I had lost too much weight living in Florida and no longer had enough body for him. These comments were clues, red flags if you will, that something in our relationship had gone left but I was blindly in love. After all, he was my rock, my promoter, the voice of encouragement when I had doubts. I completely trusted him with my heart and soul.

I was confused by what was happening so I did what I thought I needed to do to fix things. I stopped going to the gym hoping to put back on a few pounds. I stopped working overtime to spend more time with him and cooked extravagant meals after work. I went natural! And that executive position at work that had made me feel accomplished, didn't do it for me anymore. The disinterest showed and my work began to suffer. My emotional state was unstable and my confidence, shaky.

Time went on and things didn't change. In fact, things got worse and I wasn't happy anymore. The same beauty and smarts Rick used to praise was now being called "just ok". Yeah, I was still making money and climbing up the ladder of professional success but what was the point, if when I came home, I had no one to share my wins with. It all seemed pointless to me.

I didn't want the relationship to end but I was once again, lonely. I decided to leave. I wanted to move back to New York. I wanted to be around people who loved me and encouraged me. I told Rick my plans and he fought against it a bit but in the end, I left.

We were in a space where we both didn't know what we had in each other. He lived in Florida. I was rebuilding a life in New York. We flew out to see each other here and there and kept in contact but our relationship was nothing like it used to be. The love was still there of course, because connection built over years of a genuine friendship doesn't ever really disappear, so it was no surprise to me when I ended up pregnant.

With that news, I really fought for the relationship. I just knew that Rick and I would get right back on track now that we were bringing new life into this world. He was excited at first. He relocated back to New York and moved in with me. For the first four months, it was like old times. We planned a new beginning. It seemed liked this blessing was just what we needed to get back on track. I was elated. But mark my words when I say that, with that intense kind of love you not only give your partner the power to build you up, but you also give them the power to break you down.

As my belly got bigger, Rick grew more distant. He decided that we needed all the money we could get so he had to take a four-month long construction job down in Texas with his brother. I desperately wanted things to work out between us so I agreed to him leaving. I would make the sacrifice of going through most of my pregnancy alone, if it meant that our child would have a better future and a solid foundation. Rick left.

He routinely called to check on me and the baby that was growing inside of me. He sent money here and there but the next time I actually saw Rick in the flesh, I was eight months pregnant and about to attend my baby shower. I thought our reunion would be celebrated but it wasn't. He seemed so disconnected. After giving birth to our beautiful son, I still held onto the hope that we would be a family but it was all in vain. Rick informed me that during his time in Texas, he met someone new and was now in love with her.

Four months later, Rick left again but this time, Rick never came back.
Devastated, heartbroken and now dealing with the reality that I was a single mom, I gave up and let myself go.

I once looked at myself in the mirror and I used to see a pretty, smart, educated, goal-oriented woman. I kept myself in shape and was right on track with my life goals. Then I fell in love with him. His words captivated my mind. I was happy. I was in control until I willingly gave my power away. Now the person who stared back at me in the mirror was weak, scared and an isolated mess.

How did I get to this point? It didn't happen overnight. It was a slow and steady downward fall that I didn't realize happening until I was so far gone that I didn't recognize myself in the mirror. Physically, I hadn't changed much but the blatant unfamiliarity in the eyes that looked back at me was overwhelming. The peace of my soul was disrupted. I was far removed from the upbeat, driven, *ready to conquer the world girl* I used to know and love.

I didn't know this person. I had let myself become a dry copy of myself. I was blah. I was ordinary. My appearance was mediocre and my self-esteem? That was in the crapper.

I looked down at my son and then back to my reflection and decided - enough was enough. This was not who I was meant to be. This was not how I imagined my life to go. I wasn't going to let it go down that way. I was ready for a shift. I was willing to change and the time to design the life and person I wanted to be was NOW.

What happened to me, happens to countless women. I used to host a monthly book club called the Sassy Sistahs Book Club (cheesy name, I know but nevertheless) with about 40 rotating women -- and no matter what book we were discussing, the topic often shifted into a conversation about relationships. We shared stories (some of which are detailed in this book) about the hardships we went through in our relationships with men. What was absolutely fascinating to me is that no matter what age or race, we as women go through the same situations! There is nothing new under the sun when it comes to having relationship issues.

Boy meets girl.
Girl meets boy.
They fall in love.
They build a life.
Situation gets complicated.
Relationship ends.
Boy moves on.
Girl simply cannot.
She breaks down.... and very often gets stuck in the memory of what used to be.
She begins living in the past, wishing that things could be different and sadly transforms what was meant to be a beautiful life of endless possibilities of joy and abundance in love into a bitter existence of *should haves, could haves and whys*.

Why didn't I know better?
Why didn't (s)he do better?
Why is this happening to me?
Why even bother?

I want women to discover or re-discover that every pep talk, every compliment, every praise that they'll ever need is already within them. Women are a special gift to this world. We are leaders and innovators. Our love encourages, nurtures and shapes this world. Imagine a world where we not only acknowledge who we are but take ownership and use our God-given gifts for the benefit of everyone and everything we touch. We can, and should, design it that way… but we must begin with self. And this is my wish… that women from all walks of life will read on and gain a standing confidence that will improve their lives and the lives they touch -- right now.

In the chapters that follow, you will find one clear message coming through. YOU ARE ALREADY THE WOMAN THAT YOU WANT TO BE.

That dynamic woman handling her business is inside of you – maybe you've forgotten her or maybe you haven't formally met her as yet. Either way, together, our mission is to bring her to the forefront of your world so that you can choose to be her and design the life you want to live-now.

Keep reading and it will all make sense, because becoming the woman you want to be isn't about luck or pretentious behavior, it's about ownership, attitude and action.

Ownership: I AM _____.
Attitude: Confidence is key- Know it, Believe It
Action: Belief in Motion- You must do your part.

Ready? Good!

GET IT RIGHT

GET IT RIGHT
Understanding who and where you are…

The Creation: A Star is Born

Have you ever had the feeling that you were created and destined to be and do great things in this world? So many of us have lost touch with our inner dreamer. When I was a little girl, I had a fascination with diaries. I took great pleasure in writing all my thoughts down on paper. I would often do something crazy or daring during my day, just to have something to write about at night. I loved finding words to describe the inner feelings I experienced, like the butterflies I felt kissing a boy for the first time or the fright and nervousness I felt when losing my virginity. I found something so romantic about expressing myself in the written form. Writing in my diary was a daily activity and my secret joy. I shared it with no one and reveled in the privacy of it all. In that joy, I was becoming a writer before I ever considered it seriously. There was no question in my mind that I would become a renowned novelist, selling millions of books and touring the world. I imagined myself sitting on Oprah's coach, sipping coffee through a straw in my red-rimmed glasses and my red pumps. In my mind, it was a done deal. I was already the woman I dreamt about becoming and no-one could tell me differently. Needless to say, something happened along the way.

Away from home one night, my very protective (West Indian) mother decided that she would find out about what was going on in my teenage life by reading my diary. It was locked, but that proved no barrier to a woman who declared everything under her roof as hers to read, use and/or destroy if she saw fit. And boy, did mom read some juicy stories of me cutting class and going to hookie parties.

Understandably, that confrontation was one for the books. But more than just an butt-whipping, that became the night that I learned to *protect* my inner thoughts from the world. I continued to write here and there -- but my stories were now censored for fear that an unauthorized person would read them. The authenticity of my voice was diluted by fear and in that fear, my joy for writing was dimmed. Let's be clear, my mother did nothing wrong and who knows what kind of crazy, thrill-seeking life I would have had, had she not intercepted. But the truth of the matter is – my dreams of becoming a dynamic writer shifted. I focused on graduating from high school on time and I put more time and energy into studying, promising myself that I would get back to writing as soon as I got my diploma… and then as soon as I got my degree… . And that turned into… writing can wait, because I'm in love…. It seemed as if my childhood dream of becoming a famous writer became more distant as the years went by. I remembered it here and there, and kept it slightly alive with quick mental notes to get back to it -- but life somehow went on and on and on.

My point is that in life, we are all created to be great, but along the way we get off track. We lose touch with our whimsical, outrageous dreams of being THAT ULTIMATE WOMAN. Without even realizing it, we sign a "normal contract". We accept the road map to a happy life that we've been fed in school, by family and by society at large. We go to school, follow successful careers, get married and have children, all in an effort to obtain that All-American Dream. Granted all those things are commendable, and do often times bring us happiness but in that *normalcy* contract, we forget to add a *dream* clause. We forget to add the stipulation that says:

Even with life's twists and turns, we still get to be the woman of our dreams. That sexy, fun, brilliant woman, like no other woman on the planet.

Why?

We are created that way.

The Designer: Mapping Out Stardom

Design: to plan and fashion artistically or skillfully; to intend for a definite purpose; to form or conceive in the mind; contrive; plan.

The first thing I want you to understand is that EVERYTHING IS AS IT SHOULD BE. Whatever is going on in your life is happening because you have created it and/or attracted it into your world. Stuck in a rocky relationship with a man who doesn't treat you well? You attracted him. Working at your dream job? You've created that circumstance. Every delightful event, every frustrating situation, the *good,* the *bad* and the ugly has been generated by none other than (drumroll please…) YOU. You did that and the good news, is that everything is as it should be and you have the power to change whatever it is that you don't like about your world.

The first step in understanding your power is to LET GO, RELAX and BREATHE. There is no power found in fighting against what already is. The quest to try to understand why things couldn't be different creates nothing but anger, feelings of regret and disappointment. It causes an internal war between *what is* and *what could have been.* And the funny thing is- you're fighting an imaginary battle where you never win because – what *could have been* isn't real. It simply doesn't exist. Whoa…! Was that too much? Hopefully not, but I'll say it again. Whatever *could have been* DOES NOT EXIST. So let it go.

This *letting go* I'm describing is called living in the present.

When we stop resisting *what is* and stop wishing for *what could have been*, we create space for clarity and we open the door to having transparency over our life circumstances. There is a saying that I love that describes what happens when you are clear about where you are in life.

Once you see, you can't un-see.

Seeing your situation clearly gives you the power to change the circumstance. I like to call that act of choosing to change- designing. You "artistically" intend to move toward creating a different outcome in your life.

The world is in need of 'Designed Women'. These are women who choose to live their lives without apology and with great enthusiasm. Regardless of their circumstances, they live out loud and do so with a sensual grace and beauty that only a woman can exude. It is a gift given to us by the universe and we must claim it to restore balance in the world.

Think about it? What other species do you know that can be strong and vulnerable, firm yet compassionate, a beast and a gentle kitten at the same time?

Designing yourself is the key to accessing the life that you've dreamed of living. As the designer, you claim the power that has already been given by the universe to change whatever circumstances are holding you back from your destiny.

Ask yourself:

"Who am I now?" Where am I now?" then

"Who do I want to be?" "Where do I want to be?"

What steps do I need to take to get me there?

Then you can make a decision to be that person. Simple as that. I know, you're sitting there saying to yourself, "Ok crazy lady, yeah yeah, I make a choice and then POOF, I am this dynamic woman living the life of my dreams -- not buying it". And I get it. It sounds crazy but it works. Of course, once you make the decision, there is work to be done. Nothing in life worth having is given to you easily, at least not for the majority of people living on earth. But the good news is, you *can* have it – if you want it. The question is – how badly do you want it? Are you willing to design it? And are you ready to put in the work it will take to see results?

The Vow: It's Showtime!

As the old saying goes 'promises are made to be broken'. So lets call them *vows* instead. Will you make a vow to accept your life, your personal situation and circumstances, as it is right now? The decision is yours. By accepting what *is*, you tap into your personal power, the designer in you. You give yourself permission to live a life of bountiful possibilities of change and you get to choose your own path. You get to choose the relationships you nurture or discard. You get to design the type of life you live. You no longer live a life in *victim village*. You have choices. And you are free to divert from the road map society has fed you.

Let's have a look at an example of this…

Let's say you're riding in to work on the No. 5 train and, as luck would have it when you're rushing into to work, there's a signal problem on the line. You're stuck in the tunnel for an additional 10 minutes, with no cell phone service to call in late. This situation is what it is. You acknowledge that you were already upset because you woke up 15 minutes late and now this! You have two choices here:

1. You can raise your blood pressure and run the risk of looking insane to your fellow passengers by dropping the f-bomb, hitting the pole and asking the world "WHY IS THIS HAPPENING TO ME?!!"

… or …

2. You can let it go, take out your kindle and get in a chapter of that new book you've been dying to read but haven't had a chance to.

Again, the choice is yours. Letting go is where the power is. What I find absolutely fascinating is that once you let go, things tend to move in your favor. I wouldn't be surprised if that train delay resolved itself before you even got to the second page in that chapter. There is something magical about releasing negative energy and the need to react to every life experience.

Things just flow.

Wouldn't you like to see what magic can be created in your life once you accept what *is* and let go of negative energy? Make the vow.

Say it with me…"I vow to see my life, my situations, my circumstances for what it is, right now. I also vow to acknowledge and use my power to create a different outcome for my life, my situations, my circumstances. I am a designer and I choose to use my intention to artistically create the life I want to live."

Reflection Questions

1. What circumstance in your life have you been holding on to in the belief that it could have been different, *if only you… if only (s)he.. if only…?* What could change that situation if you choose to accept it for what it is in the present moment? Could you choose to design a different possibility?

2. What tumultuous relationship could you transform by designing the outcome of an encounter before the encounter?

3. How would your life be different if you gave yourself permission to design a new and improved life, based on making decisions now in the present moment?

Your Charge

For the next 24 hours, reflect on people and situations in your life that when thought of, bring an uncomfortable feeling in your being. Stop, breathe and reflect on that feeling. Try to see the circumstance for what is it and then make an effort to LET IT GO. Then choose to design a new and improved outcome. What does that look like? Get to work!

Who is the Ultimate Woman?

I've asked countless women this question and the standard answers I get range from: Michelle Obama is the ULTIMATE WOMAN, Oprah's that WOMAN or Beyonce- definitely Beyonce- she's that WOMAN. I hardly ever hear a woman say "Me! I'm That WOMAN".

I beg to ask, why is that?

Have you ever notice how easy it is to believe people's negative comments about you? And how much more difficult it is to accept and declare your positive aspects? What is that about?! Well, the time has come to make a switch from believing the negative to nurturing and acting on the positive.

Every woman has what it takes to be that ULTIMATE WOMAN – the woman they want to be. With good habits and an "I AM" attitude, you *can* be that woman you want to be. But first we have to acknowledge that there is a *hater* living in your head. That chick is loud, negative and won't shut up! It seems as though every time you have an idea that could possibly change your life for the better, like a new business endeavor or an idea to hone in on a creative talent, along comes hater!

The Hater

Come on now, we all know her... the one who screams,"Design a new life? Who? You? Ha. Brighter futures are for those people who actually get things done. Look at your track record. You have to admit, it looks a bit sad." She laughs at your ideas and she almost always gets you to agree with her. Oh, she's good.

Well, there's good news and there's bad news. The bad new is that she lives in your head. The good news is that SHE IS NOT YOU.

Try this:

For one day, pay attention - I mean really *listen* to the thoughts in your head. You'll be surprised by the on-going conversation that takes place all day, every day. The hater is usually bringing up mistakes you've made in the past or creating excuses as to why you aren't creating a better future. The answer to solving this problem would appear easy enough. All you need to do is get that crazy chick out of your head, right? Wrong. You don't need to get rid of her, nor can you -- but it would serve you to quiet her down.

How do I do that?
The first step is to acknowledge that you are not the hater. In other words, you are not your thoughts. After doing the exercise, you'll find that you are the person/being who has been listening to the hater over the course of 24 hours.

In Eckhart Tolle's book, The Power of Now, he calls you in that state of listening, "The Silent Watcher". He says: "Be the silent watcher of your thoughts and behavior. You are beneath the thinker. You are the stillness beneath the mental noise. You are the love and joy beneath the pain."

When you are beneath the thinker, you are also separated from the hater. In that separation, you can choose to exercise your will and interrupt the toxic conversation that often keeps you from exploring your dreams of greatness, of being that Designed Woman.

Sounds easy enough but the task can be quite the opposite. That hater has been running the show for years and isn't going to go away easily. Changing and/or interrupting your thoughts demands an ongoing conscious effort, and you are most easily trained to do so with the practice of **meditation and prayer.**

Meditation/Prayer

I like to think of every thought I have as being a prayer. You are always in constant conversation with God, Allah, The Being, The Universe, whatever you want to call that Greater Power. So what would your thoughts be if you knew that God was always listening to every word? Would you put yourself down? I mean, you are his masterful creation, made in his image, right?

Would you let the hater in you head shoot down all the wonderful ideas that come to you? What if they are being given to you from that Greater Power? Do you think God would be offended if you choose to believe every reason the hater keeps screaming as to why you cannot fulfill a dream that is your heart?

Let's pause here. Take some time to practice being present and connected with your inner-self and that greater power through the practice of meditation. It wont be easy at first. The hater will notice you listening and begin to turn up the noise. The conversation will get louder and more intense, but stay with it. It may take a few days but the noise in your mind will eventually decrease.

A practice guide called "Mindful Meditation" has been included in the back of this book to support your journey to presence and a quiet mind through meditation. See "Support from the Experts".

_____

"You are everything you should be with a cherry on top. You have endless power to create, design, motivate yourself into action."
- Lisa King

3 Steps to Fabulous

Step 1… Self-Awareness

The first step on your journey to fabulousness is knowing who you are and how you're portraying yourself. I call this step **Self-Awareness.** The definition of self-awareness is simple. It is the capacity for introspection and the ability to reconcile oneself as an individual separate from the environment and other individuals. In layman's terms, self-awareness is you looking within yourself and acknowledging that you are unique and that there is no one else in the world like you. This step is about finding your individuality. Becoming self-aware can be one of the hardest things to do because it requires that you be completely honest with what you see and what you find.

This reminds me of my friend, well... lets call her Casey. Casey was one of the prettiest girls in high school and stylish to boot. She easily dated any guy she wanted and she did just that until she fell in love and got married. She had a son shortly after and went about living her life. As a working wife and mother, she quickly found herself quite busy. Running around to pick up her son, rushing home to make the family dinner and keeping up with her demanding job.

One day on her way to pick up her son from school, she ran into two girls she went to high school with. They chatted a bit- catching up for a few minutes and made promises to keep in touch. But as Casey was walking away, she heard one of the girls say "Damn, what happened to her?" and the other said "Life, I guess".

Those comments hit Casey like a ton of bricks. She knew that she wasn't exactly putting much effort into her image these days, but was it that bad? She went straight home and asked her husband if she had changed much since getting married and of course, he said the typical. "No babe, you look good for just having a baby".

Side Bar:
Attention men reading this guide: That was the wrong answer!

Casey looked in the mirror and took a moment to take a real look at herself. Her hair was pulled into a messy ponytail. She wore no makeup, her eyebrows needed to be tamed, and her clothes were extremely basic. She had gained a few pounds after having her son but it was nothing she couldn't camouflage. She still held a resemblance to the girl that she used to be but Casey knew she couldn't compare.

What happened to Casey happens to a lot of women. It happened to me. As women, we become so invested in keeping up with our jobs, our kids, our husbands that we push our own needs to the back burner. Who has time to sit for hours in the salon? Who cares about nail polish when you're washing dishes three times a day, right? WRONG. You care. Your appearance is a reflection of how you feel about yourself inside. If you don't care, it will show.

What Does Your Look Say About You?

What does the clothing you're wearing, the hairstyle you're rocking and the way you put yourself together say about who you are? What are you visually giving the world? Does your look say, 'Designed Woman, empowering and inspiring those around her' or does it say "Working mom, tired and trying to make it to the weekend in one piece?" We, as people make judgments (positive and/or negative judgments) about others on first glance. Have you ever met someone and upon looking at them knew what professional industry they were in, like "oh yeah, she's probably a school teacher" or "uh huh, he's probably an athlete".

It's weird because although we make these judgments instantaneously, many of us are not aware of the message we sent out to the world based solely on our appearance. We are completely oblivious to how others perceive us. Why? We've gotten comfortable and attached to the idea that "Hey, this is me, I am who I am." Awesome attitude to have, right? Yes. I agree, but only if you're living and being yourself at your highest possible potential.

Step 2… Creating your choices

Let's go back to Casey. She had two choices here. She could either:

1. Accept the fact that the fast pace of everyday life had run her down and there was nothing she can do about it
   ---or---
2. Choose to get herself together, create an inventory list (we'll get to that shortly) and make the decision to design an image of herself at her highest possible potential.

Note: "Fine-ness" doesn't just disappear in a blink of an eye. It gradually fades away unnoticed until one day you are face-to-face with an unpleasant reality check.

Casey took an honest look at herself in a full length mirror and admitted to herself that she wasn't at 100%. She wasn't necessarily unhappy with what she saw but in her heart she knew that she could represent herself better. What did she do? She acknowledged that she had let her situation take control of her and chose option 2 and decided to Get It Right.

Where are you now?

Inventory List

Taking inventory is easy. This is the step where you write down all the things that you want to change about yourself. Grab a pen and paper and make a list of all the areas of your (physical) person and outer appearance that needs a bit of sprucing up.

Here's a sample of Casey's list to get you started:

- Body weight and fitness
- Hair, skin, nails and teeth
- Work clothes
- Weekend clothes
- Girls night/Date night clothes
- Shoes
- Outerwear
- Makeup/Cosmetics

You then flush out everything you would like to change in each area. Be very specific about the changes you would like to see.

For example, lets take Casey's 'hair, skin, nails, and teeth' inventory item.

This is how you can simply flush this out:

Hair: Healthier hair, updated style, new color
Skin: Brighter, softer, clearer skin
Nails: Regular manicures and pedicures
Teeth: Whiter teeth

If you want to really get fancy, create a vision board displaying the changes you would like to see happen for yourself. If you're not the arts and crafts type, pinterest.com is an online site that can be used to create vision boards as well.

Reflection & Action Exercise

What area of your appearance needs the most attention? If you don't know, its the one that when looked at or thought about brings about a feeling of discomfort. Work on this one first.

Do you need support? We live in a phenomenal time where everything we want to learn can be accessed with a wifi connection and a few strokes on a keyboard. Can you say YouTube? There are countless people on YouTube who are ready and willing to assist everyone from the fashionably challenged to the makeup application novice.

Is there anything in your closet that doesn't represent the Designed Woman you are creating? Let them go by donating them to charity.

"Looking good is all about using what you have to make the best of what you've got." -Lisa King

Where would you like to be?

Now that you know what you would like to change, how do you make it all happen? Details are everything when designing the new you and we're ready to move on to…

Step 3: Action…

It's time to put the work in, but don't sell yourself short. Prayer and meditation throughout this step puts you in the correct mindset to pull off this transformation. The focus it brings will aide you in taking <u>action</u> towards obtaining your goals.

Let's take Casey's body weight and fitness goal. If her intention is to lose 15 pounds before summer, meditation and prayer will get her spirit into agreement with her mind. She will know that she can lose 15 pounds before summer, but all the meditation in the world will not burn a single calorie for Casey. If she wants tangible results, she must do her part. She will need to execute an action plan to reach her goal. She could cut down on the sugar and bread she loves and hop on the treadmill for 30-45 minutes, 3 times a week or take the kids to the park and do some brisk walking. The point is that she needs a plan and she needs to execute it.

Here is Casey's Action Plan (in writing):

Goal: Lose 15 lbs, slim down, tone up
Action:

For the next 90 days
- I will significantly reduce my daily intake of sugar by removing sweets and sugary drinks.
- I will increase my water intake to at least 8 glasses of water a day.
- I will complete a 30 minute run on the treadmill at least 3 times a week.

When completed, I will feel:

Light. Strong. Healthy. Accomplished.

Meditation will aide you in staying focused on your plan but it must be backed up by your will, and executed by YOU. This is after all, your personal journey to fabulousness.

Why Women Love Her: She's Fierce

"When you look good, you feel good"-
(by Someone who knew what they were talking about)

Appearance is everything. Let's face it. No matter how much of a sexy, dynamic woman you've become on the inside, if it doesn't show on the outside -- what's the point? You've done the work. You now know how absolutely fabulous and worthy you are. Now its time for the world to see you strut your stuff. Displaying your "design" for the world to see should be approached as an art form. It should require thought and a clear vision for the way you present yourself. For those of you who think that you've got this area covered, please send your ego for a walk and continue reading…

Take for example, the dating process. I'm not afraid to admit that upon meeting a man for the first time, I check him out from head to toe. I use this overview of his appearance as a guide to accessing where our conversation has the opportunity to go.

A quick story…

One of my closest friends, Chanel, invited me along to an after work event up in Harlem. We're always looking for the best ways to connect with other young dynamic professionals. It turned out to be a pretty nice, upscale crowd. While mixing and mingling, being networking divas, I looked up to see this absolutely gorgeous man across the room. Our eyes locked for a moment, he smiled, I smiled and just like that – he walked over.

His name was Derrick, and Derrick was so very handsome. He was about 6 foot 2, of medium build, with smooth brown skin -- and the fact that he was impeccably dressed was the cherry on top. Fresh cut, clean shaven and his suit had to be custom-made because it fit him to a T! We chatted it up, laughed a bit as he reminisced about his college years at Howard University and his career now, as a Real Estate attorney. He was educated, well-spoken and was well dressed. Ok now honey, he had my full attention. He offered to get me a drink at the bar and I accepted. As he walked away, I gave him the head to toe once over, mainly because I thoroughly enjoy seeing a well- dressed man. And as I took it all in, I said to myself 'Now, there's a man who is giving the world GQ'. Until I got down to his shoes - this brother had the nerve to be wearing shoes that looked like they were on their last hoorah! I was shocked and confused. I had been swindled. I couldn't understand why this sexy, educated, professional attorney and fine specimen of a man would choose to be dapper from head to ankle.

He returned and we continued to talk as I finished my drink. But I simply could not get over the fact that his shoes looked like he was kicking buses all day. The story he was telling and the visual I was seeing wasn't adding up. Something wasn't right and although he was extremely attractive, me being the designed woman that I am, didn't have the time or energy it would take to figure this one out. So instead of accepting his offer to dinner, I politely declined, gave him my business card and made the switch from flirting mode to networking mode.

Was I being a bit shallow? Maybe.

Could I have given him false hope by taking his number with an empty promise to connect for dinner? Sure, if I wanted to be inauthentic.

The point that I'm making is that one should always give 100%. Why cut the sexy short? Don't give anyone the reason to question or doubt your stance. You are the canvas of your life and you owe it to yourself to show up and show out.

Are you a diva? Then you should be stepping out like a diva at all times. Now, I'm not talking stilettos everyday all day because divas wear flats too. Diva is an attitude - a way of life. If there is something about yourself that doesn't say diva- CHANGE IT. Simple as that.

I hear you complaining about money "A new wardrobe is not in the budget", but girl stop! You don't have to be decked out in top designer gear to be diva'd out. Its all about style and expression. I'm sure you know at least one woman that is Gucci-this and Louie-that and she still looks a hot mess! Why? Because she has no style, no self-expression. Before you head to the mall, check out your closet. You bought that cute top for a reason - maybe all it needs is a cute pair of wedges to pull it all together. Sometimes an outfit needs a lip color or a scarf to top it off.

Note: When it comes to fashion, one of the best investments we can do for ourselves is to invest in a tailor. The best look is one that looks like it was made especially for you. Your clothes should fit you perfectly. Try on outfits. Take time to complete and polish your looks. Give your appearance a lift and I guarantee that you'll instantly feel more confident about yourself overall.

Invest in Your Design

Get a Glam Squad

- Keep at least two professional make-up artists in your rolodex for special occasions or when you want an extra 'pop' to finish a look.

- Hire a professional image consultant or stylist to tangibly bring your creative visions to life.

- Find a tailor who does good work in a short time.

- Schedule routine hair, nails and grooming appointments in advance and set calendar reminders.

On A Budget?

- Watch DIY (Do It Yourself) make-up tutorials on YouTube and practice, practice, practice.

- Host a "Glam Night" where you and your invited guests experiment with different clothes, hair and makeup and styles.

- Schedule out non-negotiable "you time" to groom your hair, nails and eyebrows on a weekly basis yourself.

ARE YOU WORTH IT?

Knowing your worth is a critical part of being a Designed Woman. It doesn't matter if you're the CEO of a Fortune 500 company or flipping burgers at Burger King. You are worthy of every blessing coming your way and you deserve to enjoy your blessings without guilt or shame.

Let's talk blessings.

Take my dear friend Jenna. Now Jenna is the in-house attorney for a real estate firm I used to do HR consulting work for. She is extremely smart, super professional and has a winning, warm personality. I call her the wolf in sheeps' clothing because her demeanor hides the fact that she is a beast in the courtroom. Jenna isnt married but she's been in a live-in long-term relationship for the past 3 years. She is madly in love with her boyfriend Jay, who is her complete professional opposite. Jay has no job because after moving in with Jenna, he decided that he wanted to further his music career as a rapper/singer (think Drake). Jay doesn't make any financial contribution to the house but he is there to drop Jenna to work every morning and pick her up in the afternoon. Jenna makes a decent living as a real estate attorney and comfortably covers the household expenses own her own.

One day during lunch, I asked Jenna to take a walk with me to Saks to do some shopping. While we in the shoe department, she tried on and fell in love with a pair of Sam Edelman sandals on sale for $300. The sandals were to die for and she clearly wanted to take them.

"Girl, the sandal gods made those shoes just for you, honey. You just have to get them."
"I love them." Jenna said "but they are $300 and I dont know if I want to spend that type of money on myself."

"Huh?" I asked confusion written all over my face. "What do you mean?"

"You know, $300 is a lot of money for a pair of sandals, don't you think?" Jenna asked.

"Well didn't you just buy Jay a pair of $300 Jordans for his birthday?" I said.

" Yes, but that different. It was his birthday and I wanted to get him something nice."

"Different, how so? If you can spend your hard-earned money on sneakers for Jay, then you can sure treat yourself to a nice pair shoes just because. You're the one actually working for the money, so why not?"

Jenna grew quiet so I knew I had struck a nerve -- but hey, come on! What is the point in working hard, holding down the household if YOU hesitate in enjoying your blessings? Yes, it's a blessing to be able to treat yourself to nice things earned from the sweat of your brow. What I find about the everyday working woman is that she will not think twice about spending hundreds of dollars on her partner or child but often feels guilty about spending money on herself, even when she can afford to.

A Designed Woman puts in the work to receive her blessings and enjoys the fruits of her labor, guilt free. She understands that its not about being selfish -- its about responsibly doing for yourself what you would for the dearest loved ones.

Average Woman	Woman, By Design
Will spend $300 on a pair on Jordans for her man for Valentine's Day but hesitates to spend $300 on a pair of shoes for herself	Treats herself to nice things frequently. She works hard, handles biz and rewards herself often
Unhappy with her body and continues to live in front of the television	She is reaching her goal of optimal health and fitness
Constantly talks about what she wants out of life yet has no solid plan on how to get it	Has already decided who she's going to be, how its going to be and how she's going to get it done.
Gives up when things don't go as planned	Will never give up- ever. Revises plan and keeps pushing no matter what pitfalls she may come across
Immensely concerned about others opinion of her and because of that fear paralyzes her growth and progress	Could care less about an opinion. She is determined to be the example of what a focused mind can accomplish.
Waiting for a man to save the day	Men wish she would save their day
Pray and _asks_ God for his blessing	Prays and _thanks_ God for his blessings
Wishes she had more so she could do more	Uses what she already has to work miracles

Why Men Love Her
One word: Attitude

No matter what a woman looks like, if she's confident, she's sexy.
- Paris Hilton

Appearance is a start but that's just the beginning. If there is one aspect of yourself, which is more important and even sexier than your looks could ever be – it's your ATTITUDE.

Call it presence, call it charisma, call it swag or Je no se qua as the French do... Attitude is what sets the Designed Woman apart from her counterparts. A woman who is confident and has a beautiful personality and positive attitude can manifest anything she wants in life.

And here we're not talking rolling your neck, snapping your fingers, gotta tell everybody a piece of my mind kind of attitude. Rather the kind you exude towards others upon meeting you, that lets them know how to speak to you and how you expect to be dealt with. I call it your stance in the world and you get to set the stage.

Set the Stage
During my time in Florida, I met a girl named Kiki who couldn't understand why she always seemed to attract the same type of man. She was a pretty girl and had a nice personality, but no matter where she went

or how she dressed, the men who approached her were "suspect".

Let me explain.
I decided to go out on the town with Kiki and her friends to see what was going on. Bar-hopping in downtown Miami, the night started off like any other girls night out. We were dressed to kill, hair laid and face beat (for those of you who aren't familiar with those terms- we looked beautiful). Of course, men greeted us with the standard "hello miss, can I have minute of your time?" and "hi, can I walk with you?" Everything seemed to be in order. We continued to have a good time, drinking and giggling as we walked down the strip. Then there was a shift. As Kiki drank, she changed. She was not drunk by any means but one could say that she was a bit tipsy. It was then that I noticed that Kiki's speech changed from proper English to urban slang. No big deal, right? Right. We were having a good time on the weekend but then she began to talk loudly- like very loudly… and the louder she got, the more animated she became. In conversation with men who took an interest in her, she began to refer to her friends as "my bitches" and "them hoes" in a playful way. She then started sashaying and twirling around for her love interests to get a good view of her and encouraged her friends to do the same with "Lisa girl, aint nobody holding a candle to that shape, turn around show them what you working with." Kiki thought it was cute.

Needless to say, that our soft-spoken "hello miss" introductions, turned into men yelling from across the street "Aye yo, Red Bone, come here."

You see, Kiki's behavior, her speech and the way she chose to present herself and her friends, set the stage and told men that it was ok to approach us in that manner.

My night ended early.

"Appearance will get you noticed but confidence-true confidence from within keeps their attention." - Lisa King

Why You'll Love Her
Don't Speak About It, Be About It

I met a guy a few years ago named Danny and after going on a few dates, I was digging him. We often spoke about our life plans and the goals that we wanted to accomplish in the near future. He was working at an accounting firm as an Accounts Payable Clerk but had aspirations of becoming a fully-qualified CPA. He had taken a few accounting courses in college but hadn't quite made it to the graduation finish line. That was ok with me because hey, life can happen to anyone. You get side-tracked by family obligations or financial commitments and then before you know it, five years have gone by. What held my attention and impressed me, was the fact that Danny still spoke about his CPA aspirations in the present tense. We continued to date for months and things were going well. He was fun and I enjoyed spending time with him but there was one little thing that started to annoy me. It seemed as though, the more comfortable we became with one another, the more the talks of him obtaining his CPA died down. Whenever I would ask about what progress he's made, there was always an excuse ready.

"I missed the registration deadline to apply for the upcoming semester." followed up by "but I am definitely going next semester and when I get this license, I am going to open up my own firm. You know baby, work for myself." The daydream would continue on… complete with detailed descriptions of the vacations we would take together once that accounting firm money started flowing in. It was cute at first, to get carried away imagining the possibility of it all but after another 3 months or so... the stories became repetitive and the story, dry. I was bored.

I really liked him so I decided to step up to the role of the supportive girlfriend (and coach), by researching information about other CPA courses offerings, making phone calls and setting appointments for him. I sent him calendar invites to ensure that he wouldn't miss another deadline that would further deter him from his CPA goals. I was on top of his business -- and yet still, the excuses kept coming.

"I had to work late."

"I didn't like the counselors vibe."

Soon enough the excuses ran dry and become attacks on my interference.

"You are doing too much. I feel smothered"

"You don't trust me as a man of my word."

I chose not to take offense by his words or his tone because as a Designed Woman, I understood where he was in life. He simply was not ready. On my quest to get started on going after what I wanted in life, I often fought against myself and my supporters when they pushed me. I realize that I rejected people in my life that cared enough about me to hold me accountable for the words I spoke over my life. They became the enemy when I didn't want to take responsibility and ownership for the fact that I was at a standstill – by choice.

Danny was in that space. Unfortunately, I was tired of having more passion about his goals than he did. The daydreams that he created were no longer fascinating. In fact, the game of make believe quite bored me. He was a talker -- he wasn't a walker and so I ended the relationship.

As a Designed Woman, you'll notice that you will easily attract people in your life who have dreams and aspirations to live a big life. It's the energy you put out in the world, so it's only natural that it comes back to you. However, you'll also begin to notice that because you now have a focused mind and an unapologetic work ethic, you will become turned off when the dreams of another proves to be all talk and no action.

Choose wisely as who you invest your time into. Remember that we are on the same journey but move at a different pace. Should you choose to slow down- make sure the decision serves you in the end as well.

ENOUGH WITH THE STORY ALREADY

Another way to uncover your inner Designed Woman, is to do yourself a favor… and ditch you story, honey.

In doing my research for this book, I asked men what they found most attractive about a woman. The overwhelming response was a woman's confidence.

Meet Rich. Rich is a 36-year old finance professional in New York City. He is dark, handsome with deep, intense brown eyes. He's on the short side, at 5'8 but makes up for it with a strong, secure alpha male persona. One night at a classy winebar on the Upper Eastside, he meets Yasmine, a gorgeous naturalista with bouncing curls that danced around her face and a strong yet slim yoga instructor's body. She was stunning and they hit it off. The surface conversation flowed and the night flew by as they enjoyed each others company. Rich checked his watch and realized it was after midnight and that he had an early flight in the morning. He told Yasmine that he would love to see her again but he was ending the night early to drive back to Brooklyn. To his surprise Yasmine lived in Brooklyn too but was going to take a cab home. He couldn't let her do that now that he knew she lived in his borough. He offered, she accepted and before he knew it, Rich was dropping this gorgeous and seeming sweet woman home. He was excited but kept his cool. "This is my type of woman," he thought as he opened her car door, "beautiful, smart and she lives in Brooklyn.. sweeet."

Once they were in the car, Yasmine began to tell Rich her story, and boy did she go in! From the failed marriage in her early 20s and the crazy delusional ex-boyfriend still calling her phone, to the dysfunctional family who didn't support her dreams and the reasons she didn't feel attractive. Yasmine gave Rich the ultimate run down. She then proceeded to expose her insecurities by repeatedly asking for his opinion on her hair, her body and even the size of her forehead.

Yasmine thought that disclosing her past and her insecurities, she would instantly create a deeper connection with this man she barely knew. It did quite the opposite. Initially, Rich was beyond excited at the thought of getting to know Yasmine. She was beautiful, sexy and easy to speak to, but now he was trying to figure out a way to make it to Brooklyn in record time.

Rich zoned out and put the pedal to the metal, as Yasmine continued on. Upon reaching her building, Yasmine then on the sex, making it clear to Richard that he could come up for a "night cap". But he declined. Richard admitted to me that he felt bad because the disappointment was written all over her face -- but he did not want to lead her on, nor did he want to add ALL that drama to his life. One 30-minute ride back to Brooklyn and he felt drained, tired and fatigued. He decided to pass.

At the end of the day, no one really wants to hear your sob-story for their entertainment. Yes, you've been through some rough times in life. Yes, you may have had a failed marriage, a crazy ex-boyfriend who often stalked you. Yes, your dad left when you were 5 and your mom didn't give you enough hugs as a child. Yes, yes, yes and yes. Those things happened. Your past could be one that motion pictures are made of, and it will never be forgotten.

But, it is in the past, so let it die. It's done. Finito. Over. In this quest to unleash the ultimate woman within you, you must lose the story.

Why?
Because you are not your story. You are you now, in the present tense. What is that woman like? What kinds of food does she like? What books is she reading? What does she like to do for fun? These are topics that people (especially upon first meeting you) like to hear about because your interests give them a sneak peak into the real you.

Now, let's be clear- you cant get away from talking about your past. It will happen but you can do so from a place of reflection, not as the victim. Victims say " Look at all I've been through and feel sorry for me."

Designed Women will simply reflect, saying "Yes, that happened and I'm better for it. This is what I learned from this experience..."

Choose to speak from a place of reflection. Don't give life to the hurt and pain you may have felt during that time. Do that and you claim power over those feelings because you've grown to understand that every experience you've had, has been a lesson in some way, shape or form. You visit your past from a powerful standpoint but you know that your life is now.

Exercise & Reflection:

Grab one of your closest friends for assistance.

Do you have a story? Tell the entire story to a friend. I'm talking full details. Tell them your feelings, their feelings, how it should have been, what it could have been - one last time. Get it all out and then ask yourself, now what?

Think about how awesome it would have been to tell your friend all the things that you enjoy in life, that good book you just finished, your aspirations and vision for a better life, a better world.

How would you feel after? Would your friend feel more connected to you, the present you?

Instead of looking for sympathy by sharing your sad story, have the courage to be who you are now- not who you used to be during difficult times.

Use these daily mantras as reminders of who you are. Mantras for accessing the attitude of a Designed Woman:

I am smart.   I am sexy.   I am driven.

I'm a winner.   I am worthy.   I am enough.

I am confident.   I am whole.   I am perfect.
I am complete.   I AM ME!

KEEP IT TIGHT

Clean House- Healthy Mind

Now that we've gone through 'Getting It Right" let's get right to the task of "Keeping It Tight".

When I know that I am about to dive into a huge work project or pursue a personal goal that requires me to focus, focus, focus, the first thing I do is put on some feel-good music and I CLEAN MY HOUSE!

I am a firm believer that the condition of your home is a direct reflection of your mental state. If your home is strewn with clothes, has dishes in the sink for days and your toilet bowl is a bit…ummm… suspicious, then I can guarantee you, other areas in your life are in disarray.

Surrounding yourself with a clean home allows your mind the freedom it needs to focus on other tasks. The mind loves busy work. Notice where your mind goes as soon as you step foot into your home.

For example: If I had a report to complete for work and decided to get it done at home, I wouldn't be able to give it my attention if my home was a mess. Coming home to a pile of dirty dishes or loads of dirty laundry would distract my focus. Thoughts of "let me tackle the dishes before I settle down"… or "let me get the washing done first" would side-track me and in a flash two hours would have gone by without even having started the report.

The mind doesn't know how to differentiate between *busy* work and *productive* work. As long as it's completing a task- it's doing its job. *You* know the difference though. Give yourself a fighting chance and get to cleaning!

How a cluttered and untidy home environment can affect you negatively:

1.   **You'll feel drained.** A cluttered home can literally suck the life out of you. Stuff everywhere is a constant reminder of yet another thing in your life you haven't gotten to. The constant reminder that you have to put this away and that away brings a feeling of dread because it creates a list of to-do's that haven't been completed.

2.   **You'll feel that your life is out of control.** Why? Because the basic routines and habits that you perform and have control of – like mopping and washing, are not in order.

3.   **It can create a sense of depression.** When a person feels drained and out of control, a sense of hopelessness in attempting to correct the situation can build up and cause depression. Simply put, stuff, stuff and more stuff is overwhelming and when it becomes too much to handle, one can be psychologically frustrated.

Here are some things keeping an organized home says about you:

1.   **You're healthier.** A dirty house breeds disease. One of the biggest culprits behind many types of illness is mold -- which can grow just about

anywhere, especially in showers and kitchen sinks full of dirty dishes.

2.   **You're calmer.** Can you say WhoooSaaahhh? Most chores don't require a lot of conscious thought, so your mind has time to wander. Use cleaning time as meditation time.

3.   **You've got it together.** A clean and tidy house speaks volumes about your organizational skills.

So what can you do to improve your health, reduce your stress and keep your life in check? Uhhh, Clean Your Home- DUH!

I'm the kind of person who loves to work from a list. I feel a sense of accomplishment with each checkmark added to my list. So to help you stay on track with your Clean House Healthy Mind goal, I've included my favorite Weekly Cleaning Checklist from www.creativehomekeeper.com. I've used this in the past and it's supported me in starting and actually completing the tasks at hand.

Reflection Exercise:

After a long day at work or running errands, get present in your mind and walk into your home. How does your body feel upon entering? Do you feel a sense of comfort or does your body tense up? Where does your mind go? Does it begin to plan an enjoyable, candle-lit hot shower – or -- does it remind you that you forgot to take out the garbage?

Pay attention to your experience, and if you aren't satisfied with its direction, then take the necessary steps to clearing that negative energy. Get that checklist out and get your mind right honey!

Bedrooms	Living Areas
o Dust o Wash bedding o Vacuum/sweep floors o Disinfect door handles and light switches o _____	o Dust o Vacuum/sweep floors o Clean glass doors and mirrors o Discard "stuff" that doesn't have a place or use o Disinfect remote controls, door handles and light switches
Bathrooms	**Kitchen**
o Scrub Toilet o Disinfect Counter and Sink o Clean shower o Restock toilet paper and hand soap o Clean glass mirrors o Disinfect door handles and light switches	o Sweep and mop floors o Wipe down appliances o Clean and organize refrigerator/panty o Scrub sink and stove o Restock dish liquid o Make grocery list o Disinfect door handles and light switches
Laundry Room	**Daily**
o Clean out dryer lent o Remove clutter o Disinfect and wiper down washer & dryer o Sweep and mop floors o Disinfect door handles and light switches	o Remove and/or put away clutter o Disinfect kitchen counter o Take out the garbage o Sweep kitchen floors o Find at least 2 things to give away or throw away o Open windows for at least 15 minutes

ONCE COMPLETED, LIGHT SOME CANDLES AND
ENJOY YOUR CLUTTER FREE LIVING SPACE

Create Your Own

Bedrooms	Living Areas
o _____	o _____
o _____	o _____
o _____	o _____
o _____	o _____

Bathrooms	Kitchen
o _____	o _____
o _____	o _____
o _____	o _____
o _____	o _____

Laundry Room	Daily
o _____	o _____
o _____	o _____

A STEADY INCOME- THAT'S HOT

WORK THAT 9-5PM, DONT LET IT WORK YOU

Everyone should have a steady income and for the most of us, that means getting a 9-5pm job- at least until our true passions turn into true cash-in-hand.

There is absolutely no shame in hopping on that train and heading into that office. Even if you're current position has nothing to do with your life passion- it is commendable that you are actually working to support yourself and provide for your family.

I had a man in my life at one time that used to tell me that because I had a 9-5pm, I was a slave working for "the man" and if I didn't change that- I would never reach my goal of becoming an entrepreneur. He warned me that I would be forever condemned to a life of mediocrity, working 8 hours a day, 5 days a week to make someone else's dreams come true. Listening to this kind of talk will have you questioning your plight in life. Was I living a lie by not throwing caution to the wind, quitting my job and going after my dreams wholeheartedly? Am I giving away my precious time and energy here on earth just so I can get a steady paycheck? OMG, Have I sold out on my dreams of greatness for $60K/year and a 401K plan?

STOP.

First and foremost, consider the source. If the person that giving you these precious words of wisdom has no income, lives with his mama and the only bill he pays is his cell phone bill, then IGNORE IGNORE IGNORE because I can guarantee you, that will be the end of his advice. There will be no step by step master plan on how to free yourself from "the man" or a '30 Day Guide to Gettin' On'. Listening to rap music and thinking you know the blueprint is one thing- actually doing it and making it happen - is another.

Listen, there is nothing wrong someone advising you to go after your dreams but take advice and learn from others who have actually done it- who are living it. This is real life and to live a responsible life, one has to eat, pay rent and bills and have money to maintain a healthy lifestyle so having a source of income will definitely come in handy. As long as your dreams don't die in an effort to keep up with our 9-5pm - or - gradually fade away in the comfort and stability of a weekly paycheck then you're ok, in fact- you're winning!

Keep your aspirations and dreams at the forefront of your mind. Stay on track by using the income earned at your current job to finance your goals of entrepreneurship or whatever your dream may be. Obtaining your goals can be as simple as making a decision but what people like my ex don't realize is that with the decision to go after your dreams, comes a responsibility to yourself to MAKE IT HAPPEN by any means necessary. That is when the real work begins and it begins with you.

Get Unreasonable
When you get unreasonable and refuse to take no for an answer - you get results. Im about to get extremely corny and cliche with these lines but they speak truth:

"Where there's a will, there's a way."
"God will make a way out of no way."
"The journey of a thousand miles begins with a single step."

When you leave no room for the reasons of why you can't obtain your goals, possibilities of how can appear. Check out these examples of ways to get unreasonable with yourself:

GOAL: WHAT DO YOU WANT?

WHY YOU CANT?	WAYS YOU CAN
I have a child and he/she takes up all my extra time.	Work on your dream before he wakes in the morning or after he goes to sleep
Im too old to start a new venture- my time is up.	**GET OVER THE AGE COMPLEX-** You're here right? Someone needs that special thing you have to offer- dont disappoint them
People don't "get" me so they won't support my venture.	Who are these people, you speak of? Do they really exist? And if they do, who gives a shit about them anyway? Be true to yourself and the right people will support you.
I have good ideas but I'm not good enough to begin now... I'll wait until I'm ready.	Simply put: "The man who says he can and the man he says he can not, are both correct." - Confucious. You're enough. Set it off now.

In short, work on your dreams but girl, don't stop that cash flow. You'll have to work double time to make it happen by putting in extra time after your 9-5pm, when the kids are asleep or just before they wake up but this zest and determination to have your dream by any means necessary will give you more *life energy*.

Life Energy is that second wind you get when you push the confines of your mind. It's that extra umph, that pep in your step as you head to work knowing that you are not only holding down a job but you are that much closer to your dream.

It is a burst of creative inspiration that happens when you open your mind to the unknown. Your thoughts go from, "I don't think I can pull this off." to " I'm getting this done no matter what, so what are my options?"

Your day job becomes the foundation you need to stabilize everyday needs and a stepping stone to the next level. If you can secure your "real job" then you will surely feel more confident about pursuing your dreams.

We are all blessed with unique talents and God-given gifts. We are meant to shine and we can. The question is- How bad do you want it?

Do you want it bad enough to wake up a 2 hours early and get it in before work?

Do you want it bad enough to throw caution to the wind, put yourself out there?

Do you want it bad enough to stop caring about what others will think of you?

Do you want it bad enough to allow your dreams to scare the living daylights out of you?

If so, then all you have to do is make a decision, put in the work and witness the universe move and shift to create for you the life you want to live.

Now that you've decided that this is what you want-put the work in.

Reflection Exercise:

List a goal that you have been sitting on, unsure of how you would obtain it. Create a Get Unreasonable Chart listing the reason you can't on one side and the creative way you can, if you had to no other choice.

Remember, no one get to success on their own. Communicate your vision with family members and friends and get them involved in your journey.

INDEPENDENCE

Financial Independence is a critical part of holding your own in a relationship and in life. From an early age, women are shown movies that depict a damsel in distress, waiting from her knight in shining armour to swoop in and save her from her afflictions. That outlook is quite silly. I mean, Oh please! This chapter will let you know what can happen to you if you should ever decide to give up your financial independence.

What does having financial independence mean? This means that you are making your own money, paying your own bills and taking care of your responsibilities without the <u>needed</u> support from anyone.

Carry Your Car Fare

I remember my first date. Dwayne Drakes was one of the coolest guys in the neighborhood and he had asked me to go to the movies with him. I was so excited and went straight home to get ready. My best friend Tashica was in my room, helping me find an outfit and fix my hair- you know, typical girl stuff, when my mother came in to see what we were up to. I told her that I was getting ready to go to the movies with Dwayne. She was very protective and wasn't happy about me dating in general but I was growing up and she was allowing me to do so.

Mom sighed, made a face and told me " Make sure you walk with cab fare.".

I was confused and asked "Why? He's paying."
I know my mother did not think I was going to foot
the bill on my first date.

She said to me: "My daughter, never depend on
anyone for a ride home. I'm sure this Dwayne is a
nice guy and I'm sure you'll have a good time but as
a woman, you must always be able to make your own
way home."

This advice still rings true to date. If a woman gives
up her independence and becomes financial
dependent on a man, she'll always be at his mercy,
beck and call. A woman who works and makes her
own money keeps her dignity by having the ability to
walk away from any situation she does not feel
comfortable in. No matter what, she can make it
home.

Take Sherri for example. Sherri was dating Manny.
They met at a mutual's friends barbecue, hit if off and
began dating. Two months into it, Sherri lost her job
and was having a difficult time bouncing back.
Manny and her continued to date through this time
frame but Sherri grew increasingly uncomfortable at
dinner tables, not being able to at least offer to leave
the tip. Manny was financially able and knew of her
situation so he picked up the bill each and every time.
He never said a word.

One night, they were out on the town, having dinner
with a few of Manny's friends, another couple who
were in town for the weekend. They met the couple in

front of a famous and quite expensive french restaurant in New York City and went it to eat. Manny's temperament was a bit off but nevertheless, Sherri was enjoying the night out.

After dinner and having small talk, Sherri started to talk about the food. She never had french food before and wasn't impressed by it. "For a fancy schmancy restaurant, the food was ehhh, don't you think?"

"It was good." Manny said flatly

Sherri replied with "For their expensive prices, I should be wowed right now, don't you think?."

Manny snapped "Are you paying for anything on this table? The wine? The bread? What about the water? Are you paying for that? No? Ok, so what you are complaining about again?"

Sherri was absolutely horrified. She couldn't believe that Manny would embarrass her that way. But what made it worse was the fact that, Sherri knew that if this had happened when she was working, she would have kindly got up, thrown some money on the table, flip her hair and given Manny her ass to kiss but she was in no position to do so. She knew it and apparently so did he. Graciously and quickly, the other couple laughed the comment off, as to not make the situation worse, but the damage was done.

As long as a woman has own her resources, she will always keep her respect. What Manny did was wrong.

There is no excuse for that type of embarrassment but as a woman, my disappointed goes to Sherri.

Sherri should have know that in order to keep her respect, she needed to come to the table with something and we're talking about much more than a dinner table at a french restaurant.

In relationships, be them romantic or platonic, bring something to the table. Keep your respect. Maintain your dignity and <u>always</u> be able to walk away and make it home.

KEEP YOUR PLANS

Here's a story that proves my point.

Take Devin, for example. Devin was an attractive and successful young man. He had a professional (but cool) swag to him that easily attracted women. He could have his pick of women and he knew it, but his choice in women was quite odd. He referred to his love interest, Tandi as the " techie secretary-type" (who wore ballerina flats with everything). He liked her and after a few dates, he booked a hotel stay and flights for them to enjoy a weekend away in Miami together. Now mind you, Devin was the cat's meow and booking flights without asking a woman if she could make it wasn't a concern for him. He just knew that Tandi would jump at the chance of spending a fun, romantic weekend with him.

On their next date, Devin surprised Tandi with the tickets by cooly saying " by the way, I took the liberty of booking a trip for us next weekend. We're going to Miami."

Devin watched her closely, awaiting an animated squeal or jump of excitement but it didn't happen.

Tandi smiled, looked up from her plate and responded "Really, that's too bad because I already have plans."

Devin was shocked to say the least. He almost choked as he sipped his water.

"What do you mean plans?" he asked.

"I have a brunch scheduled with some girlfriends. Sorry but I wont be able to accompany you but you have fun."

"CANCEL!" Devin thought but he was way to smooth to seem affected. He tried a different approach, describing the glitz and glamour of the hotel, the jet skis they'd ride and the amazing hotel pool.

Tandi listened but didn't change her mind. Devin told me " I couldn't believe that she was telling me no. There is no way in hell that a woman would pass up an all-expenses paid trip to sunny Florida for the weekend. Another man must be occupying her attention." Devin ended up cancelling the flights in order to take her out to a movie on the Friday night. On the Sunday morning, he decided to wake up early and drive past the brunch spot Tandi mentioned she and her girlfriends were going to. In his mind, her rejection of him, had to be because of another man.

Devin threw on a Yankee fitted, a hoodie and some sunglasses and went cruising by the brunch spot (yes, men stalk too). Sure enough, Tandi and one of her "friends" were sitting in the restaurant's window. From the car, he couldn't tell if she was dining with a woman or a man so he decided that he'd randomly take a stroll past the restaurant. As he was passing, Tandi looked up, their eyes connected and Devin was frozen in time.

Tandi looked pleasantly shocked, waved at him to join her. Too embarrassed to refuse, Devin went with the flow and entered. She introduced him to her best friends and asked the waiter to pull up a seat for him.

The point being made, is that instead of laying out on the beach in sunny Miami, Devin was caught somewhat stalking a woman and had managed to crash an all-girlfriends Sunday brunch. All because Tandi decided to honor her commitment to her friends.

Devin recalls some of the thoughts going through his head at the time. He said "Here I am, super swaggy young man and somehow I landed myself as the only man at a table full of women talking about relationships. It was quite comical. This woman had me unknowingly swallowing my pride and from that point on, I knew she was the one."

Some readers may think that Tandi should have ditched her friends' brunch or at least attempted to reschedule it for the following weekend. I mean, damn…! What kind of woman wouldn't mind a man whisking them away to sand, sunshine and blue ocean water?! The answer is a woman who is self-assured as to what she brings into a relationship. Tandi didn't need or want validation from Devin on any part of her life. She made a choice to stick to her plans and figured that a man who had balls enough to make a decision on her behalf, without checking with her first, had some pretty big kahunas and could handle a little rejection. He took a gamble and she chose herself in that situation. He got that, and it blew Devin's mind. Her self-assurance and confidence intrigued him and their relationship strengthened as he came to appreciate and admire her strength.

Another woman with self- esteem issues may have been completely impressed by Devin's gesture and excitedly gone with it. Don't get me wrong, sometimes things come up at the right time, in the right place and we all, indeed do only live once. But a woman's constant readiness and continuous availability makes the stock value of spending time with her plummet at an extraordinary rate.

In this example, Devin took a gamble and Tandi choose herself and choosing yourself is one of the most attractive things you can do as a Designed Woman.

It shows that you put worth and value into what matters to you most. Choose you and others will too!

GET YOUR LIFE

I've seen it time and time again. A woman gets a man and suddenly, he becomes her life. She becomes obsessed with being the perfect girlfriend -- the "wifey" type. She can't have drinks after work with her girls because she has to run home and make dinner. She doesn't know if she can hang out this weekend because she wants to make sure he doesn't have plans for them to spend time together. All of this, and its only six months into the relationship. Listen up ladies, STOP THE MADNESS!

Truth: Men love it when you have a life of your own. Think about it. Would you want to have a man who acts like a puppy dog waiting for you to return home from work? If you had a man who was waiting for your approval before he made a decision.... you would label him as weak. And slowly but surely you'll start to disrespect him or even worse, start finding other, stronger men more attractive.

Take the line from Jay Z's song for example: "Where'd my girl go? Oh, on world tour". Exaaactly. Men take pride in bragging about all the things their woman has going on in her life. Who doesn't like to have bragging rights? You see the same behavior with mothers and their children. Proud mothers won't think twice about telling the world that their child has made the honor roll or got into a gifted program. It all boils to pride and I'm not talking about the pride you feel before the fall -- I'm talking about the pride that makes your heart swell with joy.

The personal relationship with your other half is no different- men and women alike love to talk about what an intelligent, gifted, ambitious, self-driven person they have on their arm. It's a reflection of who they are. The old saying goes "show me your company and I will tell you who you are".

Well, the point is that a Designed Woman continues to live her life as she normally would. If she had always gone to the gym three times a week- she'll continue going to the gym three times a week. A good relationship doesn't take away from her personal life *per se*, but adds elements of passion, adventure and eventually love. She never stops being her, because after all, that's who he's interested in.

For example, my good friend, David was dating a woman named Carolyn whom he had met in the gym. He saw her from across the room, as she ran on the treadmill. She had her headphones in and she ran with intensity. David says, " she looked so focused and that intrigued me". Although he was done with his workout, he lingered about the gym waiting for her to finish hers so that he could have an opportunity to talk to her. After about 20 minutes, she was done and he made his move. She was friendly and engaging so he asked her out. She accepted.

They went on a few more dates, their phone calls became more constant and everything seemed to progressing smoothly. Until he noticed that she wasn't in the gym anymore. When he asked her about it, her response was "Oh, I haven't been there in a while, I have much more fun hanging out with you- the gym can wait." David was immediately turned off. Although he liked Carolyn, her choice to switch up her lifestyle because of him was a red flag and a turn off.

What Carolyn failed to realize is that the intensity and driven the demeanor she displayed at the gym was the initial attraction. That's what actually drew David in. Her saw her intensity and focus and he had to find out more about her. Take that away and it spells needy, insecure and flaky.

In his mind, Carolyn would rather give up her personal goals (no matter how minor they might be) to do what she thought was pleasing to him. It almost always has the opposite effect.

GOT A LIFE? NOW, KEEP A LIFE

It is imperative in the dating and courtship world, to always keep a man guessing. When things start becoming a bit routine, switch it up! Never get too comfortable with the status quo.

The more predictable your routine is, the easier it is for a man to become turned off. In the previous story about Tandi, you can replace brunch with any number of events, and rest assured that a man's ego cannot comprehend that something else can be chosen over his company.

He'll be asking himself "Why would she want to do that, when she could be hanging out with me?" My advice- let him keep wondering. When a woman drops everything to be at a man's beck and call, she appears desperate to be in a relationship. Saying no, every once in a while, re-establishes your position as worthy and at the same time, he will begin to pursue you again.

Be Unpredictable
Married and single women alike, spend too much time waiting on a guy to either call or ask them out, and it doesn't necessarily put them in a position of power over the situation.

A married girlfriend of mine named Karen, took this "switch your routine" advice for a test run when she started to feel that her husband had become too comfortable. You know the story… less dinners out and date nights, no more surprise bunches of flowers. He was a workaholic and she often found herself waiting by the phone after work to see if he would be making it home or if was choosing to work overtime. Karen often turned down offers from co-workers to go and grab a Happy Hour drink because she didn't want him to come back to an empty home. And many a time when she turned down an offer she found herself home alone anyway, because he decided to take his co-workers up on their offer to connect after work. She loved her husband but felt taken for granted.

Feeling like she'd had enough, Karen decided to shake things up at home. How, you may ask… by staying one step out of his reach. She'd finished up at 5pm and called to tell him that she wasn't going straight home because she was having a quick bite to eat with her co-workers. She'd leave for work in the morning and wish him a great day but wouldn't follow up with a "make sure you call me when you get there and on your lunch break". When he called her, she picked up for the most part- but sometimes she purposely didn't answer because she was "unavailable".

The first time that Karen wasn't available for his call, Jeff went beserk. He called at 5:15pm and got her - she said that she would be hanging with the girls after work and would see him when she got home but didn't specify what time that would be. They hung up and it took everything out of Karen to put her phone away and not text or call Jeff with updates of her night. She made a conscious effort to enjoy herself. As the night went on, Jeff noticed the silence of his phone and thought that it was weird that Karen had not checked in at least every 30 minutes to an hour. He constantly checked his phone, until after two hours he decided that something had to be wrong and he called his wife. The phone rang and then went to voicemail. Getting no answer, he continued to call every 30 minutes until Karen eventually decided to pick up at 9pm.

With music in the background, Karen greeted him with a cheerful "Hi Baby?"

"Oh hey babe, whats' up? What are you doing?" he responded.

"What do you mean? I'm still out with the girls. Everything ok?" Karen said distractedly -- but she was only half-listening, giggling and still chiming in on conversations being had at the table.

To her husband, she sounded like she was having a good time and he was happy for his hard working wife, but he couldn't help feeling as though she might be having a bit too much fun without him. A tinge of jealousy overcame him, he admitted.

"Yes, yes...everything is ok. I just wanted to check on you. See you soon."

"Ok hun, bye." and Karen hung up.

"Love you..."

She stayed another hour before leaving, making it home just before 11pm. To her surprise, Jeff was still up, watching television, apparently waiting for her to come in (although he'll probably never admit it). He looked happy to see her and gave a big hug and kiss as he whispered, "I miss you" as she walked in the door.

Before, Jeff could set a clock by Karen's routine, and he took her presence for granted –someone who was always there, at the same time day after day. One night of switching it up gave Jeff a much-needed reminder that Karen didn't have to be there every night. She chose to be there and now with the revelation that Karen had a life outside of the relationship, Jeff suddenly missed her. Their time together seemed more precious; her presence, something to be appreciated.

The point is that, as women, we must never stop having a life of our own. Take a class, go back to school, learn to sew or join a gym (and actually go). Whatever interests you have outside of your relationship should continue to interest you during your relationship. The mere fact that you enjoy living the life that you have is attractive in itself. Being quite content with or without a man's company, be it your husband or not, keeps you… desirable.

ALL WORK.. NOW LETS PLAY: Burning Up Baby!

Ok Ladies, let's kick the fellas out of the room and have some girl talk. Lets talk love. Lets talk body. Let's talk sex. Lets talk YOU!

Love Your Reflection

I was sitting in my doctor's office flipping through an edition of Glamour Magazine when I came across an article called "**Shocking Body-Image News: 97% of Women Will Be Cruel to Their Bodies Today.**" It sounded interesting enough so I decided to read further. Let me say that I was absolutely shocked by their study. In a survey of more than 300 women of all sizes, research found that, "on average, women have 13 negative body thoughts daily—nearly one for every waking hour. And a disturbing number of women confess to having 35, 50 or even 100 hateful thoughts about their own shapes each day." - Glamour Magazine

I thought to myself, "Do I love my body?" and surprisingly I had to think about. My answer wasn't "YES!" right away. It took some convincing, I found myself forcing an affirmation "Yes Lisa, you love your body." but then came "I could tighten up the stomach area" and " Yes, I love my body but a squat or two wouldn't hurt."

DING! I realized, in that moment, that I could have easily been a statistic in Glamour's case study. Well,

111

you know being the Designed Woman that I am - when something comes up for me, be it an insecurity or belief- I simply must examine it closely. So I went home and got completely undressed. I then went and stood in front of a full length mirror and stared at myself. At first I felt silly. I shook my head and giggled thinking "Girl, you are nuts- put your clothes back on and get started on dinner" but I fought against it.

asking a couple deep breaths in, I focused my attention on becoming present.

I stared.... and I listened and stared some more.

I realized that my conversation about my body image started off positive but the more I stared, the more the conversation shifted to my imperfections, like my stretch marks along my lower belly and the way my breast had changed after breast feeding.

Clearly, I wasn't as confident in my body image as I thought was so my goals became to:

1. Change the conversation I subconsciously have with myself in regard to my reflection into a positive one.

2.   Change whatever it is that I am not satisfied with on my body by creating an Inventory List and Action Plan.

I made it a non-negotiable task every night to stare at my naked body and have positive conversation with myself about what I saw. I also started to work out to get started on the change I wanted to see.

Here are my suggestions on how to change your body image conversation:

1. **Rewire your brain.** If you know that constantly thinking negatively about your body teaches your brain to focus on the bad stuff,- Flip the script! Make a conscious effort to compliment yourself.

2. **Ask yourself: Is this *really* about my body?** If it is, then make a list of what you would like to change and how you plan to get it done. If not, think about it. When you say 'I am so FAT!" Do you really believe that or are you comparing yourself to unrealistic image of what society says a beautiful body should look like?

3. **Exercise!** Research shows that people who worked out regularly tended feel better about themselves and have positive conversations about their bodies to others. Physically active improves your shape and health; and it also boosts your mind-set, too. One new study found that women felt better about themselves after exercising even when their bodies didn't change.

Reflection Exercise:

Complete the mirror exercise. Listen to the conversation that you're having with yourself about your body image. Dont like it? Change it.

SEX- This is a must!

A healthy sex life is an important part of living your best life. Sex is a gift that should be enjoyed equally by both partners. Too many times, women get carried away with the idea that their main purpose in bed is to "please the man". They go into the bedroom ready to give a stellar performance, yelling "Yes! More, More, More" and sex become a show.

Sex should make a woman feel loved, special and last but not least - empowered. You are a woman. You are a prize, made with deep valleys and hidden secrets that captivate men. Your bodies hypnotize, our sexual aura scoops men up and our orgasms are enriched with a passion that drives men absolutely crazy.

When women have orgasms during sex, men feel like superman- their testosterone doubles and the champ in them emerges. Bringing a woman to her peak gives their confidence a boost, so the best thing you can do for a man in bed is enjoy yourself.

Who knew, sex is all about you!

The key to making this happen is to:

   1. **Be comfortable in your skin and with him.**
If you are not totally comfortable with a person in bed. I mean take a up close look at it comfortable, 'Baby, I like it like this' comfortable, "look into my eyes while we do this" comfortable- then maybe, just maybe you shouldn't be having sex with that person.

Good sex is about comfort and communication so make sure you have that foundation in place before diving it. There's nothing worse than awkward sex.

2.   Learn your body and be honest.
You should know your body better than anyone.Don't buy into the "He can't make me climax" bit. The truth of the matter is that- You can't make you climax. Learn to please yourself so that you can teach others how to do so. Trust yourself and him. Voice your likes and dislikes (nicely) for a more satisfying exercise.

3.   Relax and Let Go.
Every woman deserves the right to have the best sex of her life each and every time she engages in the act and if you're not having an orgasm - then there is a mental block that you must acknowledge work it out and try again. Remember, sexual energy is creative energy so free your mind for an awesome experience.

Studies have shown that a healthy sex life coupled with frequent orgasmic pleasure can actually make you a healthier, happier and younger looking person.

A younger appearance: As sex increases the blood circulation, it helps pump more oxygen to the skin which results in a brighter complexion that even continues following that well-known after-sex glow.

Improves sleep: You may have noticed that you sleep better after having sex. Research has found that the oxytocin released during orgasm helps induce sleep.

Better mood: That's a given. Think about the office, you can tell who's getting it on the regular and who might need a quick pick me up. If you can't think of anyone, you might be that girl.

Keep Up With Your Lifestyle and WORK IT OUT

We're all a teensy bit guilty of having unrealistic expectations at the gym: a few squats and presto—one size smaller! Nothing works that fast, but with the right strategy you can see results in just two weeks, says Nikki Skeete, trainer and founder of SkeetElite Fitness of Orlando, Florida. What makes that possible: Eating a healthy diet, of course and while you're at the gym, remember to focus on muscles that respond fastest to strength training—those in your arms, shoulders, calves and lower abs.

At Home Tone It Up Workout

Jumping Jacks or Jump Rope

5 -7 minutes to get the heart rate gong.

Squat and Shoulder Press
Works thighs, butt, shoulders

Stand with feet hip-width apart holding five-pound weights in each hand, arms bent, palms facing in. Bend knees and squat, pause, then stand and press arms straight up over shoulders. Do 8 to 12 reps.

Crossover Lunge
Works calves, hamstrings, butt

Stand with arms at shoulder height, palms down. Step forward with right foot, crossing it in front of left. Lower into a curtsylike lunge (right knee shouldn't go past toes) while twisting torso right. Untwist, push off right foot, return to start. Do 8 to 12 reps; switch legs and repeat.

Walking Plank

Works abs, chest, arms

Bend forward, place hands on floor in front of toes, and walk hands forward, until you reach plank position. Do a push-up, then inch back to start. (Keep belly button pulled in.) Do 8 to 12 reps.

Side Plank

Works abs, obliques, butt, hips, thighs

Lie on right side with legs extended, hips and feet stacked; prop yourself up on your right forearm, elbow under shoulder, and place left hand on your waist. Slowly lift hips off the floor as high as you can; hold for 15 to 30 seconds, belly button pulled in toward spine. Lower to start, switch sides and repeat.

Killer Legs and Butt Workout for the Busy Woman

20 squats
30 lunges
40 standing calf raises
50 second wall sit
100 jumpn jax
50 second wall sit
40 standing calf raises
30 lunges
20 squats
30 second Plank

Nikki says: "The key to seeing results with this workout is to go full blast and all the way through-NO STOPPING. If you are a beginner, you're allowed one water break after the jumping jacks. Breathe, finish strong and stretch before and after your workout. Not intense enough? Double and triple up your reps. No time? One minute PLANKS throughout the day, goes a long way!"

This workout, done morning and night is sure to get those legs and butt looking RIGHT in no time. Now lets get to work!

For more information on Nikki Skeete

visit: www.facebook.com/nicoleskeete

IG: @skeetelitefitness

"FRIENDS"

Haters.
Everyone has them.
Know how to handle them or they'll handle you.

They are usually the people who sit, judge and criticize from the sidelines. Those kinds of haters are obvious and apparent.

However, there are hidden haters as well, lurking around, mixing and mingling in your circle. Some of them may be newcomers; some may have been in your face for years.

The worst thing you can do for a hater is be humble and low key. A woman who is secure within herself doesn't feel the need to convince anyone of her worth because her presence speaks for itself. It's seen in the way she carries herself, how she treats others and most of all, how she treats herself.

We, unfortunately live in a world of competition. It saddens me to say that some people get it into their heads that if you are doing well and treating yourself as a Queen, that that somehow takes away from their worth.

You know the scene… you enter a room with your friends… you're looking good… and no one gives you a compliment. You lose weight or you make over your hairstyle completely… and no one says a word.

Do not and I repeat, do not doubt yourself. You've created your image and it's exactly what you want. Do not get upset about the noise and definitely don't feel uncomfortable with their silence.

As a Designed Woman, you run your show and you must be confident in the decisions that you make -- be it a hairstyle, a new career path or a partner.

We as human beings, often look for validation from loved ones. We want our families and friends to be happy for us and to give us a pat on the back for have a job well done. When we don't get it, it can be felt as rejection and shake our foundations. We may start to question our position and our ability to know what's best for us. But through prayer, meditation and good old fashioned faith in that greater power, the voice in your head will become the loudest voice you hear -- and that is when you have mastered a life, By Design.

This is so much bigger than just your physical image -- this is about finding yourself within yourself and truly having the audacity to live as yourself.

And when insults happen -- don't take them personally. They are a gift. They're given to you to teach you. They bring forth insecurities so that you recognize them and make the choice to overcome them.

You get mad because you believe that there is truth in their statement. Be aware of your body's reaction to an insult. Are you getting hot and angry inside?

Before you react, acknowledge that emotion and ask yourself if their statement is true. If not, let it go. If you find the slightest bit of truth in their statement, you owe it to yourself to take a look at the issue.

As a woman living your life by design, I encourage you to be selective with who you surround yourself with. Be with people who have the same value in friendship that you do. That decision will only serve to forward you on your journey.

3 Friends that Every Woman Should Have in Their Circle:

1. **The Supporter:** This friend is there to root you on and keep you shooting for the stars. She is the listening ear when you feel as though you want to give up. No matter what you're circumstances look like - she will find a solution and suggest possibilities of 'making it work". She increases your vision with her 'do more, keep going' attitude.

2. **The Analyzer:** This girl is the supporter with an edge. She will listen to your dreams and goals. Encouraging you all the way through BUT has a technical mind that aides you in finding creative ways to overcome obstacles to ensure that can make it happen realistically. She bring the vision into focus.

3. **The Pusher:** This friend isnt afraid that tell you what they see. You will often feel

uncomfortable in conversations because she calls out arrogance and ego when they show face in your life. She is the friend that you will often argue with because she is your mirror. She will show you the ugly within yourself but will do so with love.

Secure women can and most definitely should be friends with one another. Being confident in your worth and position in the world removes jealously from any situation.

In my many years of leading open discussions and conversations with women, I've heard it all. "I should be getting what she's getting." "Her success is based on luck - not talent." That's the hater in your head talking and she will limit your blessing. These are conversations I like to call "Lack" conversations and they do cause a lot of lack in your life. Lodged in these comments is the belief that if a woman is highly successful aka winning, that somehow others (you) are losing.

Women, check the hater in your head and adopt the conversation of 'overflow." Overflow says: THERE ARE ENOUGH BLESSINGS IN THE UNIVERSE FOR EACH AND EVERY ONE OF US TO WIN. Understand this and watch your success increase beyond your wildest dreams. The human mind, all of the 10% percent that we use cannot even begin to conceptualize the favor that waits for us to catch on.

CLAIM YOUR QUEENDOM

"Heavy is the head that wears the crown."
Shakespeare

CHANGE YOUR CONVERSATION

In your quest to claim your Queendom, you must understand that "with great success, comes great responsibility". When it comes to the way you live your life, the way your treat your loved one and the audacity by which you go after your dreams; lukewarm is no good, kind of passionate is for the birds. You must reach for the stars with red-hot passion and vigor. It's the only way to live the life you dream of. Receiving what is meant for you, your great blessing, is going to need you to change your conversation -- mainly the one that you have with yourself.

Here are a few on-going conversations you should have with yourself -- starting NOW.

1. Your life, your decisions
The opinions of others are of no consequence when you stand in your truth. How others see you does not hold a candle to how you see yourself. We are all on the same planet, sharing the same space and time and truth be told - none of us truly know what we're doing. As long as you honor the sacred part of yourself and keep it real- what's real for you, you are already braver than most.

Some may refuse or reject you because unapologetic truth is not the most comfortable thing to stand before -- but real recognizes real, and you will not be alone. Be authentic. Be genuine and be perfectly ok with not being perfect.

Trust yourself more than you trust others.

2. Fall in love with your dreams
The key is to align your heart with your mind. The most important decision you make every day is how you will spend the limited amount of time you have been given in this life. No matter how old you are and where you are in your life, you get to dream. Place your thoughts and vision into the things that bring you joy and then go after them. Dream big, lavish, extraordinary dreams and fall in love with the vision you see. Go after them with great might and passion.

3. All your wins count - Be Grateful
On your journey to greatness, thank God for small mercies along the way. In other words, be grateful for the little victories in life. Lifelong happiness is not found in one colossal jump to the mountain top, but in the slow and steady climb. Feel blessed by each step you take and enjoy the view on the way up.

4. Serve the world
This reminds me of one of my favorite quotes by Ghandi. He says: "the best way to find yourself, is to lose yourself in the service of others". Yes! Your life is so much bigger than you. Get clear on what your impact will be in making this world a better place.

Your presence is needed and the world is waiting for exactly what you have.

Make it a practice to get up and ask yourself, what can I give of myself today that will make the world a better place by putting a smile on someone's face? Selflessness is contagious and begins with you. Be the example. Change the world.

5. Claiming Your Queendom? Be specific.
Remember that when it comes to living a life by design -- you must be clear. Be very specific in what you want as well as what you are willing to give up in order to get it. When you make a decision to go after your dreams, keep in mind that everything and everyone can't go with you. You will have to make tough decisions, but if you listen to your heart and choose with a sound mind, you will make good decisions. Pray for discernment and trust your inner wisdom.

CHANGE YOUR CIRCLE

I know, I know… who needs a section on friends when we've chosen them wisely our entire lives. Our friends bring us nothing but positivity, rays of sunshine and happiness. After all, we've been taught that "you are the company you keep" at a very young age.

Take a look around you, I'm sure everyone in your circle is setting goals, going after their goals, lending a listening ear when you need one, and cheering you on along your journey to greatness. Right? Ha!

REALITY CHECK!

In a perfect world that would be the case, wouldn't it? As you choose to live a life by design and claim your Queendom, not everyone in your "circle" will be happy for you. Do not get offended, because both you and I understand the impact of the amazing things you are up to and how it will make a difference in your world, and consequently, in theirs. People who are unhappy with themselves simply cannot be happy for others. Do not judge them because you may be further along in your journey but pray for them and hopefully, they will catch up and understand that in this game called life- everyone can win.

Reflection Exercise:

Make a list of the people in your life who you consider to be good friends and family. These are the people you spend the most time with. For each friend or family member, I want you to list the positive impacts they have in your life. Then alternatively, list the negative impacts they have on your life. DO NOT RUSH THROUGH THIS PROCESS. Take your time and evaluate what your close friends and family bring into your life. Start with the person you spend most of your time with, and then branch out. Reflect on how each person uses their time with you. Do they talk about their lives? If so, is it in a positive way? Are they passionate about life and their direction in it? Are they doing something that is meaningful to you? Do they complain a lot? Do they talk about other people? What is the general feeling that comes up when this person is thought about?

Hey- these people aren't on the execution line of course. This is just a simple exercise to determine where your influences are. If you are spending time with friends and family who aren't necessarily bringing you guidance and inspiration, then maybe, just maybe you might want to take a look at that. People don't get to stay in your circle just because they've always been there.

Personal growth requires one to change -- changing your habits and belief systems, as well as changing the influences.

How do I get started? I mean, these are my childhood friends, my people.

Changing your circle is not about kicking your people to the curb and 'chucking the dueces'. Your people will still be your people if they respect your mission. Leave the ego at the door and every once in a while, check in to show that the love is no less and the respect you have for them is still at the utmost.

Surround yourself with people who are speaking your language. Seek out those who are doing the things that you are, or aspire to do. Make a coffee date with someone who is successful in the ways that you want to be. The people you choose to associate with will be who you become. Make every friend in the circle count.

More benefits associated with changing your circle:

1. **Extends your reach:** Meeting new people gives you the opportunity to meet even more new people which spells out network and connection.

2. **Feeds your creativity:** New influences, in conversation alone will feed your creative mind.

3. **Expands your vision:** With your extended reach and your creative juices flowing, your vision has no other choice, but to expand. It's inevitable.

CHANGE YOUR CIRCUMSTANCES

People are always blaming their circumstances for what they are. I don't' believe in circumstances. The people who get on in this world are the people who get up and look for the circumstances they want, and, if they can't find them, make them.

George Bernard Shaw, Irish playwright and a co-founder of the London School of Economics

This quote still rings true to date. The way you choose to deal with your circumstances in this moment is determining the outcome of the circumstances in the future. The power of change lies within the decision you make now, in spite of what your situation looks like.

It's our perspective that holds us back from changing our circumstances.

Take this statement for example: " My circumstances prevent me from pursuing my dream."

Hmmm. Think about this for a minute. What's preventing you? Circumstances are facts. Facts with opinions are excuses.

"My car is in the repair shop." That's a fact. Got it.

Add: "so it's making me get to work late" and there you have an excuse.

There is no ownership or responsibility in that statement. It almost sounds like you're campaigning for a spot in victim village. Excuses help us get out of taking action and gives us a reason to wash our hands of the situation because it just too big of a circumstance to overcome.

At this point of the book, we know that's complete bull. That mindset will keep you dis-empowered and immobile. Circumstances are real but they become paralyzing when we attach emotion to the facts.

1. **Accept the facts**: The circumstance is what it is, in the moment.

2. **Ditch the emotional baggage**: Lose the tears and the sob story you've attached to the situation.

3. **Get to work:** Give yourself permission to go beyond the circumstance to find your next step.

It may take one powerful move to change your circumstance or it may be several small steps, but the point is get moving and keep moving. You can get it done.

CLAIM YOUR CROWN

In order to have a Queendom, you must reign as Queen. Stand strong and do not fear the responsibility.

As women, we have to be responsible for where our minds take us. We are filled and blessed by our emotions, our compassion and the way we can love like no other being on this planet. We often get carried away, losing ourselves and our identities in caring for others -- but we are queens.

We set the stage for our respect. We are responsible in our love and we live our lives, by design.

If you need a reminder of your crown, repeat after me:

I believe in myself.
I am worthy.
I am good enough.
I am a Queen.
I am here and I am ready to live my life, By Design!

Believe in yourself, having faith in the Greater Power and live an audacious life - on purpose!

Remember: "If faith, the size of a mustard seed is all that is needed to believe that all your dreams are possible- then a little audacity is energy needed to transform those dreams into reality." -Lisa K.

SUPPORT FROM THE EXPERTS

MINDFUL MEDITATION with LINDSEY PEARSON

Lindsey Pearson is Mindful Meditation practitioner and coach in New York. She offers guidance and practical tools to working professionals, stressed out teens, and hedge fund managers. Visit her at <u>www.doyoumindfully.com</u>

Mindfulness is a pretty popular buzzword these days. Everyone at Google, Facebook and Huffington Post are using these 2,500 year old tools. So what is it? It's being PRESENT to your own experience in REAL TIME and WITHOUT JUDGEMENT. *Hmmm...got it...wait...what?*

Our brains operate on two levels. The Narrative and the Direct Experience. The Narrative is the story...*"What am I doing with my life?" "Why didn't he call me?" "I can't believe she said that!"* It's the regret of the past and the anxiety of the future. Neither of which we have any control over. If beating ourselves up over past choices and worrying constantly about future situations garnered any results, we'd have heard about it by now. The Direct Experience is what's happening NOW. (I am drinking tea, it is warm in my hand, it smells like cinnamon, it tastes sweet) We spend so much time multitasking, we rarely check in to what is happening right now and the NOW is the sweet spot. By training our brains to focus on the present, we engage a new muscle that reduces anxiety and depression. But like a muscle, we have to practice using it.

Here is an exercise you can try right now:

My Presence is Present
Sit comfortably in a chair or on the floor with your back supported. Take a few deep breaths in a way that feels natural. There is no need to breathe specifically through the nose or for any set length- just be easy with it.
Start to check in with your senses. Notice what your hear in/outside the room: You might hear an air conditioner, outside traffic, the subway whirring along. If there's a loud or distracting noise, try not to get irritated or create a story of it ("Dang kids, I TOLD THEM! I am MEDITATING!"). Just notice there is noise and come back to your senses (literally). Take notice: What do you smell? Perfume? Food? A Pet? Take a moment to check in with your sense of smell. Next, what do you see behind closed eyes? Spots of light? Patterns? Visions? Now what do you taste? Your last meal or ? A mint? If you get lost in the story about your last meal or the next one coming...come back. Now check in with how you feel physically- tired? alert? Are you hot? Cold? Do you have any aches or discomfort? Are you hungry? Tired? How do you feel emotionally? If you're sad or anxious, can you acknowledge how that feels in the body without judging it?

I hear you asking: "What do you mean by acknowledge but don't judge?"
Let's take this situation for example:

Let's say you called your ex-boyfriend to rekindle the relationship and he blows you off. Naturally, you're devastated in the moment.

There are two different ways we relate to ourselves and our experience, with and without judgment. There are called the Narrative Experience and the Direct Experience.

Narrative Experience: *"I pissed off and sad because I SWORE I wouldn't call him again and I did and now look what happened!!! How could I be so stupid?!*

What is wrong with me."

Direct Experience: *I feel sad.... My chest is tight. My eyes are burning. My breathing is short and rapid. My blood is pounding in my skull. My stomach is in knots.*

You might say....why would I want to acknowledge all that? Sounds painful...but funny enough it is quite the opposite.

When we acknowledge how we are feeling without adding the unnecessary layer of self- judgment, more often than not the ill- feelings pass. When we beat ourselves up, we compound the damage by dragging our whole emotional system on a roller coaster which leaves us exhausted and drained. We do more damage when we don't acknowledge what's happening at all or lie to ourselves about what we are experiencing. I call that the "I'm FINE Syndrome". We deny our mind and body the healthy process of feeling our experiences in a healthy or timely matter so we shove the feelings back down and we become a time bomb waiting to explode.

By checking in with ourselves and letting the feelings wash over, **we take our power back** and no longer have to fear feeling unpleasant emotions. We know they will pass.

Much To Do About Karma

Loving Kindness is a cornerstone of Meditation traditions and is a great tool for letting go of resentment and cultivating forgiveness. Many of us have been hurt and are often told to "pray for them". ***But I don't to! I want them to hurt like I did!*** Well, much like worrying never changed an outcome, wishing evil doesn't create instant Karma for them, it just weighs us down and poisons us from the inside. We lose our power by letting this person control our thoughts and emotional well being. So lets take it back, shall we?

Loving x 3

Pick **3** sentences that resonate with you and your wants/desires.
Example:
"May I be happy"
"May I be healthy"
"May I have peace"

These phrases can be anything...inner strength, love, a calm mind, free from danger...choose your own adventure! Once you pick these phrases, repeat them to yourself **3** times. Picture yourself as though you were experiencing each word....happy...healthy...peaceful.

Next you will picture someone you love and you will repeat the phrases in your mind to them:

May you be happy
May you be healthy
May you have peace

Then...the 3rd person. They are what's called "the difficult person". Maybe its an Ex, or a boss, or friend who burned you. If someone just popped into your head right now....that's the one.

May you be happy
May you be healthy
May you have peace

When we do the Loving x 3 Meditation in order we first offer a gift of kindness to ourselves, which for some of us is a very rare experience. We would never speak to others the way we speak to ourselves. So take this opportunity to feel what it's like to be kind to yourself.

When we say it to someone we love, we are filled with gratitude for that person. A smile comes to our face. A warmth may surround us. We may begin to open our hearts.

When we practice saying these words to the "difficult person" we can start to let go of anger towards the other person by creating a space of forgiveness and healing.

But don't take my word for it- Google it! Studies have shown that by practicing this style of meditation for at least 8 weeks we increase feelings of joy, happiness, and hope, We decrease anxiety, migraines, chronic pain and PTSD. In the immediate, while we are saying the words, the body's systems relax themselves. There is even some evidence it slows the aging process!!

Sound good? Try it.

Love Notes, Quotes and Affirmations
from Lisa K.

"You are worthy of all God's blessings- and the crazy thing is - you don't even have to ask for them. They're already waiting for you. Thank him and claim them."

"No matter how bad it gets, there is always a choice to be made."
"A woman should know her worth, like she does her shoe size."

" We are all blessed with unique talents and God-given gift. We are meant to share them and we can."-

"Know your craft. Learn it, study it, know it inside and out. Communicate your vision with raw passion and flawless delivery." Lisa King

"Genuine people are magnetic. They draw others in with their "realness". Why? Because people can sense when someone is taking on a personality that isn't theirs. The truth of the matter is, when you are comfortable in your skin- it creates an atmosphere that encourages others to be comfortable in theirs."

Know your truth.
Speak your truth.
Live your truth.

LA FEMME DEVINE

I wrote this poem and performed it at the July 2014 "Lets Chop It Up: Love and Communication" discussion. Many of you asked for a written copy so here it is. Enjoy!

La Femme Devine
(The Divine Woman)

I am confirmation of your greatness
Affirmation in your time of weakness
I am strength in a gentle embrace
I am THAT woman.... Love Passion Grace

I see you- the real you
Your dreams, aspirations and goals
In the midst of doubt, I present your crown
And whisper "My King, be strong, be brave, be bold"

The calm found in fury when my arms hold you tight
I am the voice that strengthens your spirit
Words of abundance, and eternal life

I'm a soldier- I am peace
I am soft - I'm a beast
I am woman... The Woman Devine
I am your truth... and you...you, My King
You are mine.

Mine to feed, nurture and watch grow
Uplift, uphold and hopelessly love forever more
You see, Ring or no ring, I choose and the deal is done
I'll be your moon and you my bright shining sun and
I rejoice in emotion, get caught up in all the commotion
A rhythmic whirlwinds of passion and devotion..
My soul... it scoops you up and just like that
Just like that... your logic interrupts

It interrupts.. It interrupts... us.
Now you call my love crazy
Saying a love like this couldn't logically be
No, never could it be a possibility
Now, you don't know how to love La Femme Devine

And so...
You betray me and I spit fire.
Shake your foundation, destroy your empire
I see the deception in your eyes
before your mind even formulates the lie
And I cry... like why?

Now Your absence and neglect got me feeling like I
hate ya
I'm thinking united states, court , judges and pieces of
paper
I'm on the phone like "Girl, fuck the moon and stars
This negro gon' pay this child support or that ass gon'
behind them bars"

Baby? My King?
Why you acting like you can't see
Fronting like we can no longer be
Determined in your quest to no longer love...
La Femme Devine
Don't you know?!

I mold boys into men, men into kings and KINGS!
into humble servants of the One who reigns supreme
Yet you- refuse to acknowledge my divinity
You use and abuse and mock my femininity

You reject my gifts and have the nerve to call them insanity
(and whats even crazier is that..)
I still see you and long to once again capture
The days when I loved you with no until's- just the ever after

My heart breaks..and my soul.. it aches... when you turn and you walk away
But like judgment day, so close yet so far away...
You'll reach out for me
Grasping at the memories of the used to be you and me
Truly blind, can't see

All because you chose, you chose, you chose not to love
A woman... like me.

BY DESIGN

ISBN:978-0-9863662-0-8

:

ABOUT THE AUTHOR

Lisa King is the Editor-In-Chief of
www.ALittleAudacity.com and the creator of the "Lets
Chop It Up" Relationship Discussion Series. She lives
in Brooklyn, New York with her son, Isaiah.

For more information, send inquires to
info@alittleaudacity.com

Made in the USA
Middletown, DE
31 January 2015